SECTION 504

A LEGAL GUIDE FOR EDUCATORS

Practical Applications for Essential Compliance

Assessments • Staff Development Tools

Case Law • Issues & Answers

Christina Sepiol, JD, EdD

Published by
PESI Publishing & Media
PESI, Inc
3839 White Ave
Eau Claire, WI 54703

Cover: Matt Pabich
Editing: Bookmasters
Layout: Bookmasters & Amy Rubenzer

ISBN: 9781559570305

Library of Congress Cataloging-in-Publication Data

Sepiol, Christina, author.
Section 504 : a legal guide for educators / by Christina Sepiol.
pages cm

ISBN 978-1-55957-030-5

1. Children with disabilities--Education--Law and legislation--United States.
2. Individualized education programs--Law and legislation--United States.
3. United States. Rehabilitation Act of 1973. I. Title.

KF4210.S47 2015
344.73'0791--dc23

2015027196

PESI
Publishing &
Media
www.pesipublishing.com

Introduction

The treatment of individuals with disabilities and the evolution of a legal arena known as disability rights has been a journey that, in many ways, has paralleled the Civil Rights Movement of the 1960s. The initial attitudes and practices used with the disabled were grounded in deep division and segregation. Both physical barriers and mental attitudes served as obstacles to their integration and acceptance into society. Over time, much effort has been put into changing the understanding of the general population relative to the worth and contributions of disabled individuals. Today, the inclusion of people with disabilities into society and their right to gain equal access are still goals that are both relevant and challenging. One role of the school environment is to promote, model, and implement systems to ensure that disabled students' rights are not compromised. This requires a continuous level of supervision and monitoring. Today's special education staff need to have a solid understanding of the legal foundation behind their systems so as to maintain legal compliance and drive future decision making that affects those with disabilities.

Section 504 of the Rehabilitation Act of 1973 ("Section 504") is one of the legal strongholds in the quest to give disabled individuals equal access to the educational benefits offered by our public school system. Coupled with the mandates of the Education of All Handicapped Children Act in 1975, thereafter renamed the Individuals with Disabilities Education Act (IDEA) and later reauthorized as the Individuals with Disabilities Education Improvement Act of 2004 (IDEIA), disabled students are entitled to a free, appropriate public education (Public Law 94-142). Even though the combination of these two federal laws should be enough to safeguard against disparate treatment, practices still exist that have a discriminatory effect. Going forward, schools need to focus on measures that:

> Assist our educational system in identifying those actions that have a discriminatory impact on disabled students; and
>
> Develop procedures and systems to protect the rights of disabled students in the school environment.

This legal guide is designed to provide you with the legal framework for understanding the fundamental concepts that serve as the foundation for Section 504. Equally as important, this resource is designed to give you practical guidance on implementation and decision making relative to compliance with Section 504. As your level of familiarity grows with respect to the law and its application, the likelihood is that your 504 Plans will be better developed, your 504 conferences will be more successful, and you will be able to identify and correct those practices that serve as obstacles to the disabled student in the school environment.

This valuable resource will assist you to:

1) **Become familiar with the legal concepts and protections as found within Section 504.** The language of Section 504 will be broken down into its component parts with a focus on the purpose and goals of this civil rights law. To exemplify its application in the school environment, case law and other legal guidance will be reviewed to enhance the relevance to you and your staff.
2) **Identify the qualifying conditions that warrant the development of a Section 504 Plan.** Given that one of the most common questions fielded from staff centers around which students are eligible for a Section 504 Plan, the qualifying conditions and process for establishing the actual 504 Plan will be outlined.
3) **Determine the difference between the need for a Section 504 Plan and an Individual Educational Program (IEP).** Both the IDEIA and Section 504 will be examined for similarities and differences. Most importantly, staff will receive the guidance they need in order to determine when a Section 504 Plan is warranted and when the situation requires an IEP.
4) **Identify the procedural requirements and safeguards under Section 504.** The language of Section 504 contains distinct procedural requirements. Safeguards also exist for the protection of the student and parent. Knowing these requirements is critical to compliance and avoiding future conflict.
5) **Identify and proactively address common issues facing parents and school staff with regard to Section 504 compliance.** Confusion about Section 504, including its parameters and boundaries, is not uncommon. Identifying potential problems before they surface helps to address misperceptions and misinformation about Section 504. Proactive strategies will be outlined that will assist you in this regard.
6) **Outline record keeping requirements.** Section 504 has record keeping requirements that your staff will need to know as they go forward to ensure compliance under the law. An overview of ways to be proactive and establish records procedures will aid them in this important task.

Table Of Contents

CHAPTER 1

A Legal Foundation for Understanding Section 504

"Ignorance of the law excuses no man."

John Selden

A number of factors challenge today's school staff teams and speak to the ever-changing nature of education. These factors include, but are not limited to, high-stakes testing, research-based interventions, school safety, progress monitoring, curriculum, and the seemingly endless introduction of both federal and state mandates that increase our obligations in the classroom. Keeping abreast of these changes becomes an important component in delivering high-quality education that produces students who are able to compete in our global economy. In fact, one may argue that a student who has not received instruction that is relevant to the times we live in has been disadvantaged on a number of levels. For example, they may not be able to compete successfully against their peers in the areas of employment or have the opportunity to gain admission to postsecondary education at the college or university level. The responsibility of school staff to adjust to current trends and follow legal mandates is a vital component in the formula for student success.

For school staff members who are responsible for the education of students with disabilities, the interplay of various legal mandates and the awareness of relevant updates to the law require constant supervision. When legal guidelines are revised, school staff must interpret those changes with a focus on their application in the classroom and school environment. The implications of new legal obligations must also be considered and shared with general education teachers and administrators. A constant vigilance is necessary to not only provide quality educational programming but to ensure that the rights of disabled individuals are protected.

Civil Rights Laws and Their Purpose

Before dealing specifically with both the fundamentals and nuances of Section 504, we must have a basic understanding of the purpose behind civil rights laws. Civil rights laws, generally, are designed to promote fairness and equal treatment. Put another way, civil rights laws are meant to "level the playing field." If you think about a level playing field, a football field for example, all players should have the same footing. Everyone should be playing on the same ground. We would not expect that one football team have a smooth, grassy field and the other team have a field that has a ditch running through it and the rest of the field is full of holes and large rocks. Anyone seeing such different fields would conclude that any competition between the two teams would not be fair. Clearly one team would have an advantage over the other. The basic purpose of civil rights laws is to make sure that several different categories of people, one of which includes people with disabilities, have a "level playing field" or an equal opportunity to play.

Another important factor in understanding the purpose of civil rights laws is that they are focused on opportunity. They are not designed to give an advantage. In other words, the fairness concept of a level playing field does not extend to giving one team a head start or points that they did not earn. For example, the disabled student should be given an equal opportunity to try out for the football team, but it does not mean that he will automatically make the team. The purpose of the law is to ensure that the individual has an opportunity, or "level playing field," in which to compete with nondisabled peers for the chance to show off their football skills. This opportunity is only fair and is what civil rights laws are designed to accomplish.

Enforcement

The enforcement of Section 504 is the responsibility of the Office for Civil Rights (OCR). Their enforcement scope extends to any program or activity that receives federal financial assistance from the U.S. Department of Education. Section 504 provides:

> No otherwise qualified individual with a disability in the United States . . . shall, solely by reason of her or his disability, be excluded from the participation in, be denied the benefits of, or be subjected to discrimination under any program or activity receiving Federal financial assistance. (29 USC § 794)

The Office for Civil Rights also enforces Title II of the Americans with Disabilities Act of 1990 (ADA). Under this law, OCR ensures that discrimination is not being practiced in state and local government services, programs, and activities (including public schools). Under the ADA, the prohibition against discrimination is in force regardless of whether the entity receives federal financial assistance.

When OCR becomes involved in a case, it usually stems from the complaint process. Parents, student advocates, attorneys, or any party believing that discrimination is occurring may file a complaint with OCR. Upon receipt of the complaint, OCR reviews the complaint and may decide to conduct an investigation. These investigations may take the form of a records review, in-person interviews, or both. After completion of the investigation, OCR issues a letter that is sent to the parties. If discrimination is found, a letter of corrective action outlines the measures that will need to be taken in order to remedy the situation. A remedy may require that staff engage in professional development or draft new procedures/policies to eliminate the discriminatory practices. Proof of compliance is then submitted to OCR by a certain date so that the matter can be concluded.

An OCR investigation can be a lengthy process. It can require a tremendous amount of data collection and staff time in order to prove that discrimination is not occurring in your school environment. In addition, if OCR encounters other practices they believe may constitute discrimination, they can extend their investigation to those additional issues. OCR is not limited to the original complaint issue.

Finally, you should be aware that OCR's investigation and enforcement authority is not limited to complaints involving the discrimination of the disabled. OCR also addresses complaints alleging discrimination based on race, color, and national origin under Title VI of the Civil Rights Act of 1964. It enforces the Age Discrimination Act of 1974, which prohibits discrimination on the basis of age, and Title IX of the Education Amendments of 1972, which prohibits discrimination on the basis of sex. Lastly, it enforces the Boy Scouts of America Equal Access Act, part of the No Child Left Behind Act of 2001, which prohibits denial of access to or other discrimination against the Boy Scouts or other Title 36 USC youth groups in public elementary schools, public secondary schools, local education agencies, and state education agencies that have a designated open forum or limited public forum.

As the attorney for a high school district, I had the opportunity to counsel them through an OCR investigation involving an allegation of discrimination based on race. Specifically, a fight involved two groups of girls that were believed to be in rival gangs. The school conducted a thorough investigation into the factors leading up to, and including, the fight. Each group of girls was given disciplinary consequences. The parents of one of the groups of girls filed a complaint with OCR alleging that their daughters were given a harsher consequence because of their Hispanic ethnicity. OCR took the complaint and requested all documentation of the investigation, including the consequences given to the other group of girls. This type of documentation was relatively easy to compile and the district felt confident that the records would prove that no discrimination existed. However, much to the district's surprise, OCR extended their investigation into the disciplinary consequences of the entire district. For a three-year period, the data from all disciplinary referrals, broken down by race, had to be gathered and organized. Because a typical disciplinary referral does not contain racial information, a clerical staff member had to access this information from the school's database. This activity was extremely time-intensive. After all the information was amassed, I prepared a report that outlined the data and defended the district's actions. Although the district obtained a favorable finding from OCR that no discrimination had occurred, the time, effort, and funds expended to achieve this result were substantial.

Protected Class

Before we can engage in whether a practice or policy is discriminatory, we must first establish that the person(s) is in a protected class. Simply put, the law prohibits people from making decisions about others or treating people differently solely because they fall within a certain category. These categories are known as protected classes. Even though our focus is on the protected class of disabled individuals, we are aware that other protected classes include race, national origin, religion, sex, and age.

The purpose of OCR is to ensure that protected classes of people are "protected" from discrimination. They ensure that their status (as a protected class) does not impede their right to have a level playing field in their environments where they learn, live, and work.

Discrimination

We now know that civil rights law within Section 504 is enforced by the Office for Civil Rights. We further know that one has to be in a category of a protected class before we can even consider whether an act or practice constitutes discrimination. But to truly understand the purpose and scope of Section 504, one must have a solid understanding of the concept of discrimination.

The word discrimination itself carries with it a harsh and negative connotation of exclusionary acts meant to disadvantage a particular group of people. As it applies to students with disabilities, it evokes images of practices that are mean-spirited and degrading. In today's society, no one wishes to be accused of discriminating.

Unfortunately from a historical perspective, discrimination of students with disabilities was not considered as prohibitive as it is today. In the case of *State ex rel. Beattie v. Board of Education of the City of Antigo*, 172 N.W. 153 (Wis. 1919), the Wisconsin Supreme Court supported the exclusion of a student with a disability from school because he produced the following:

> . . . a depressing and nauseating effect upon the teacher and school children [and] that by reason of his physical condition he takes up an undue portion of the teacher's time and attention, distracts the attention of other pupils, and interferes generally with the discipline and progress of the school.

The court went on to support his exclusion by stating:

> The right of a child of school age to attend the public schools of this state cannot be insisted upon when its presence therein is harmful to the best interests of the school. This, like other individual rights, must be subordinate to the general welfare.

Although the court's opinion was written in 1919, discrimination continued to be the topic of controversy 35 years later in the landmark case of *Brown v. Topeka Board of Education,* 347 U.S. 483 (1954), when the Supreme Court ruled that the practice of school segregation did not give an equal opportunity for education. Although not specifically addressing the issue of disability rights, the court's statement supported the concept of the right of disabled students to have equal access by stating that "in these days, it is doubtful that any child may reasonably be expected to succeed in life if he is denied the opportunity of an education. Such an opportunity is a right which must be available to all on equal terms" (347 U.S. at 493, 74 S.Ct. at 691).

Nearly 20 years later, the court was still grappling with the topic of discrimination in the case of *Pennsylvania Association for Retarded Children v. Commonwealth of Pennsylvania,* 343 F. Supp. 279 (1972). In this case, disabled students were being denied admission to school unless their parents could contribute to the cost of educating them. The court's ruling that this practice violated the Equal Protection Clause was instrumental in initiating the change that would be required for the passage of the Rehabilitation Act of 1973.

According to *Black's Law Dictionary*, discrimination is defined as:

> A failure to treat all persons equally where no reasonable distinction can be found between those favored and those not favored.

This definition is yet another way of expressing the notion that people must be afforded a level playing field.

As an example, I received an inquiry from a high school district client that had a large population of deaf students. The students were involved in after-school clubs, sports, and activities. In order to participate, they required sign language interpreters. As a result, the expense (to the district) of paying multiple interpreters to go to the games, competitions, and activities was mounting. This expense was one that had not been contemplated for budgeting purposes. They called me and asked if they could limit the deaf students to two after-school clubs, sports, or activities. Wanting to make a point, I told them that they could definitely make that limitation as long as it was applicable to all of the students in the entire district. The district responded that they would not think to limit all the students, to which I replied that they could not limit only the deaf students. I explained that the decision to limit participation was solely due to the students' status as members of a protected class (disability) and that it would constitute discrimination. Without any ill will or malice on their part, the district did not initially contemplate this decision as one in which they would be discriminatory; they viewed it as a budgetary decision. Nevertheless, an understanding of the types of practices that can constitute discrimination was necessary in order to avoid an outcome that was ill-advised. So as you go forward with decisions regarding your treatment of students with disabilities, your guiding principle should be whether you are offering them an equal opportunity when compared to the opportunities given to nondisabled students.

Discrimination: A Review of Practices

Today's discriminatory practices, especially in the field of education, are rarely the result of malice or an intent to harm. In most cases, it is simply a lack of awareness that different treatment can constitute discrimination. The following examples are practices that you will want to consider to protect against discrimination:

Shortening the school day for students with disabilities

Rationale: Disabled students are entitled to a free appropriate public education under Section 504. This entitlement is for a full day of instruction. If you are practicing early release due to transportation issues or a more fluid dismissal procedure, such practice can be considered discriminatory. The reason that it could be considered discriminatory is because at the core of your decision is the student's status as being disabled. In effect, the disability is the reason for the different dismissal procedures. If the Section 504 team (which includes the parent) decides to institute an early dismissal or late arrival procedure, a discussion should include ways in which the missed instructional time can be made up.

Putting restrictions or conditions on participation in class field trips or activities (the message that "you can't go unless your Mom goes") when such conditions are not applicable for all other students

Rationale: Although students with disabilities may present with behaviors that are challenging or conditions that warrant close adult supervision, their participation in class field trips or activities must be identical to those opportunities given to nondisabled peers. As an example, a student who needs a nurse with them during the school day will also require that same level of support while on a community outing. Excluding the student because the nurse cannot leave the building or is reluctant to go on the trip would not be the same opportunity as afforded to other students and would therefore be considered discrimination.

Separate honor rolls, recognition ceremonies, or graduation ceremonies

Rationale: The existence of a separate system for recognizing the accomplishments of disabled students constitutes discrimination because it singles them out as having a disability. This level playing field concept is not one anticipated in the law. Students with disabilities should be eligible to receive the same academic and extracurricular awards and recognition as their nondisabled peers.

Students who attend an alternate school or receive their education at a different location may have the opportunity to participate in a separate graduation ceremony at that site. This type of participation is not considered discriminatory. However, the student should also be afforded the option of participating in the graduation ceremony at their home school in order to avoid the appearance of discrimination.

Mandatory seating arrangements for students with disabilities at such functions as school assemblies, concerts, holiday programs, or graduation

Rationale: Singling out the students with disabilities into a certain section of any assembly of people is obvious discrimination. They should have the option of choosing their seating in the same way that other peers are choosing where they sit. Of course, it is not discrimination if a student's need, as outlined in his Section 504 Plan or IEP, requires special seating. As an example, a student in a wheelchair may require access to the front row in order to see the speaker or stage, which would not constitute discrimination. However, making the decision to seat the fidgety student with ADD at the back of the assembly where he can disrupt the fewest number of people would not be acceptable. Students with disabilities who choose to sit with each other because they are in the same classes with each other and are friends would not be an example of discrimination. The central question to ask when deciding whether a seating arrangement is discriminatory is whether the disabled student has the same seating options as all other students.

Conferring a different diploma for students with disabilities

Rationale: The type of diploma that a student with a disability earns is an important topic to discuss with parents. In some cases, the parents may wish their child to earn a certificate of completion or receive a certificate of attendance. As the family cares for the student into his/her adulthood and accesses outside support/funding for this purpose, the document indicating how the student completed high school may become an important factor.

What would be discriminatory would be to categorically decide that all students with disabilities should only receive a certain type of diploma or certificate. This decision should be made on a case-by-case basis.

Modifying class rank or other criteria to restrict students with disabilities from earning the same recognition as their nondisabled peers

Rationale: All too often I have heard general education staff protest that students with disabilities taking special education or modified coursework should not be on the same class rank as their general education peers taking honors or advanced placement coursework. Their main concern seems to be that the disabled student will achieve a higher class rank than the nondisabled student. I have heard that this situation is not "fair" because the level of coursework is so dramatically different.

Students with disabilities are working on material at their level. They are working to their capacity, just as other students are working to their capacity in an advanced placement or honors class. The measure of recognition should not be based on the difficulty of the material but on the accomplishments and achievements of the student. The level playing field, and what we are celebrating with our recognition, is student effort and achievement.

The Office for Civil Rights, *in Letter to Ickes* 305 IDELR 50 (OCR 1989), gave guidance on honor roll placement and approved the use of a weighted grading system that assigns a lower grade weight to special education courses. The act of weighting the grades must be made by an assessment of the course content, and not a categorical decision.

Indicating a student's special education status on a transcript

Rationale: In 2008, OCR put out guidance entitled In Report Cards and Transcripts for Students with Disabilities, 51 IDELR 50 (OCR 2008) that outlined the parameters for grading and transcripts for students with disabilities. In that document, OCR was clear that any notation indicating a student's special education status or receipt of a special education service or related service would be considered discrimination.

Put another way, any person reviewing a transcript should not be able to ascertain whether a student has a disability. This type of information or designation serves no purpose. Likewise, if the person reviewing the transcript reads the titles of the courses and can ascertain that the student took special education coursework, it would be considered an act of discrimination. Your coursework titles should not contain words that indicate special education status. Examples of words that would indicate special education status may include, but are not limited to, *modified*, *functional*, *life skills*, *basic*, and *special education*. The only way that these words may be acceptable is if you also use them to designate some general education classes. The practical approach that many schools employ for their own record keeping procedures is to numerically code special and general education classes differently. In this way, the numeric coding system is only known to those people who are in the school system; any other person reviewing the transcript will not know of a student's status. In this way, you are creating a level playing field.

Locating all special education classes in a designated area or hallway

Rationale: Discrimination is grounded in the practices of exclusion and isolation. Placing special education classes in a separate hallway or designated area of the school building can easily be interpreted as an effort to exclude disabled students from their peers and the school environment. Although many actions do not have this intent, school staff must be vigilant against making decisions that could be interpreted as an attempt to exclude students with disabilities.

Preferential Treatment and the Parent Perspective

Another form of discrimination that is rarely the subject of controversy, but occurs nonetheless, is the practice of giving the disabled student preferential treatment. Preferential treatment, in and of itself, is an extra bonus of sorts. It is typically not necessary and is done with good intentions. Think of preferential treatment that you may have experienced: not having to wait in line, being given an extra serving of food, or having someone offer to help you lift a heavy item. These gestures are usually unexpected yet appreciated.

Preferential treatment for students with disabilities, done exclusively because the student is disabled, can be interpreted as discrimination. Take for example the situation in which you see a blind person who is about to cross the street. You decide that you will assist the person. Although you have good intentions, you are making the decision to help before knowing whether the person is capable of crossing the street independently. Your decision to assist is based solely on the fact that the person is disabled. Imagine your surprise when the blind person speaks sharply to you and tells you to mind your own business! Your gesture was not based on the needs of the individual but was a categorical decision based on the person's disability status—the very definition of discrimination.

In the classroom, staff members need to be mindful of this type of discrimination. Students with disabilities should be given the opportunity to learn, even if it involves a certain amount of struggle, alongside their nondisabled peers. Certainly if they require assistance it should be given to them, but categorical treatment should be avoided. This type of discrimination is sometimes harder for staff to identify because the thought behind the action is perceived to be beneficial for learning. As an example, seating the disabled students in the front row (when their Section 504 Plan or IEP does not call for this accommodation) may seem like a good idea. However, it may actually single them out if other students are not also told where to sit. Best practice or just good teaching strategies become discriminatory when they are only practiced with students with disabilities.

Parents of students with disabilities can be extremely vigilant regarding the perception of discrimination. They cause us to look at school practices, procedures, and decisions with a new perspective. Parents have been known to raise the issue of the equality between special and general education classrooms even as it applies to the square footage and the number of windows in the room. Their mission is to ensure that their child has a level playing field.

Case Study : Preferential Treatment

Joey

Joey was a student who required a minimal amount of resource room service and speech therapy minutes. The staff was fond of Joey and wished for him to succeed. As a result, they often allowed him to spend extra time in the resource room. Due to some of Joey's fine motor problems, they even ordered him a stamp with his name on it so that he did not have to struggle to write his name on his paper throughout the day. The staff felt comfortable in planning for Joey's success and giving him this level of preferential treatment.

When Joey's mother found out about all of the extra service that her son had been receiving, she was upset. Without defining it as discrimination, she explained to the staff that in order to accurately plan for the level of service that was appropriate for him, he must be afforded the opportunity to succeed or fail on his own. She accused them of not fostering his independence.

The staff quickly came to realize that their efforts, while grounded in the best of intentions, were discriminatory in nature. As a result, they eliminated some of the preferential treatment. Ultimately, Joey still needed support, but he surprised the staff with some of his compensatory skills. He grew to be a more independent learner, and the team had better data to plan for future services.

Case Study : Discrimination

Billy

Billy had just received a cochlear implant, which was new technology for the time. At the same time, the parent-teacher organization (PTO) had completed its fundraising efforts for new playground equipment. The group was in the process of choosing the equipment and mapping out the playground configuration. Billy's mother heard of the planning and shared that Billy could not go down a plastic, spiral slide. The static produced from going down the slide could permanently affect his implant. The school offered to have staff on the playground to prevent Billy from going down the slide. The parent alleged that this would constitute discrimination, because all other children were not prohibited from accessing the playground equipment.

The parent wanted the PTO to install steel slides. The PTO had planned to install two slides anyway, so they offered to make one a steel slide and one a plastic, spiral slide. The parent said that her son should have the choice to go down any slide that he wanted, just like the other children, and thus both slides should be steel. She argued that other children were not limited in their choice of slides and neither should her son. Ultimately, both the PTO and the school decided that the relationship with the parent was more important than the choice of slides and so the decision was made to install two steel slides.

A group of parents of special needs students believed that their children were arriving at school on the bus at the same time as their nondisabled peers but were being held on the bus. They believed that the nondisabled peers were being immediately released to go into the school while their children were retained. They believed that such practice constituted discrimination. In fact, the reason for the retention was to ensure that necessary support staff was present to escort certain students who needed assistance off of the bus. When the school was notified of the parents' concern, they addressed it. The school district had not made intentional efforts to treat the disabled students differently from their peers.

Discussion Questions

The following are hypothetical situations for you and your team to consider and discuss. Important points and answers to each situation are outlined in Chapter 6.

Situation #1 **Sexual Discrimination?**

As you walk into the conference room, a sign directs you to sit in one of the front rows if you are male, because males usually have a tendency to leave early for both scheduled breaks and at the end of the day. Hopefully, sitting in the front row will decrease this temptation.

Is this discrimination?

____

____

____

____

____

Situation #2 **Smoker Discrimination?**

You are on a job interview and are asked if you are a smoker. When you answer "yes," you are told the interview is over because the company does not want to hire any smokers.

Is this discrimination?

____

____

____

____

____

Situation #3
Preferential Treatment?

Your school requires staff to be in their classrooms by 8:00 A.M. every morning. A teacher comes to you and shares that she has a daughter with a disability who takes medication. By the time the medication "kicks in," the bus has left and the daughter has to be taken to school by car. This results in your staff member coming to work at 8:20 A.M. Your staff requests this accommodation but you want to decline it.

Is this discrimination?

____

____

____

____

____

Situation #4
Religious Discrimination?

You hire the best applicant for the job but later learn that she is Catholic and will be observing all of the religious holidays and holy days of obligation. You fear that this will interfere with her attendance and attention to her job responsibilities. You want to tell her that you have changed your mind regarding her employment and that another job applicant was more qualified for the job.

Is this discrimination?

____

____

____

____

____

Situation #5
Hair Color Discrimination?

Your advanced placement physics teacher begins the school year by telling the students that the material in the class will be quite difficult to understand. He asks all blondes to come and sit in the front row. He promises to speak slowly to them and repeat directions frequently.

Is this discrimination?

____

____

____

____

____

Situation #6
Disability Discrimination?

You are the building administrator for a special education program for students with behavioral challenges. The program has a physical restraint component. A required duty of all staff is to participate in physical restraint techniques. In the process of hiring a new teacher, it is shared with you that the applicant has a disability that precludes her from participating in any physical restraint procedure. You decide that you are not going to hire this particular applicant.

Is this discrimination?

____

____

____

____

____

See Chapter 6 for a legal analysis of these situations.

CHAPTER 2

A Legal Foundation for Understanding IDEA

"Our challenge is not to educate the children we used to have or want to have, but to educate the children who come to the schoolhouse door."

H. G. Wells

The Individuals with Disabilities Improvement Act of 2004 (IDEA) is another federal law that is critical in understanding the legal rights of students with disabilities. The IDEA has undergone several reauthorizations, resulting in more substantive changes over time as compared to Section 504. For staff addressing the needs of students with disabilities, both laws are important factors in providing legal protections.

In a subsequent chapter, the distinctions between Section 504 and IDEA will be outlined. For many concepts, the principles and protections remain the same. What follows is a discussion of the framework behind the legal principles of this significant piece of legislation.

Free Appropriate Public Education

A Free Appropriate Public Education (FAPE) is the term used to describe the educational opportunity that should be afforded to all students with special needs. What that term actually refers to and its exact definition are at the heart of every team meeting, every discussion, and every conflict. The delivery of a FAPE is as individual as the students served in the school setting. For some students, FAPE consists of a multitude of intensive supports and services. For others, FAPE only requires a minimal level of intervention. The goal behind the concept of FAPE is to level the playing field for students with disabilities.

The landmark case that exemplifies the FAPE concept is *Board of Education of the Hendrick Hudson Central School District v. Rowley*, 458 U.S. 176, 102 S. Ct. 3034, 73 L.Ed.2d 690 (1982). In this case, a deaf student by the name of Amy Rowley was being served in the general education setting.

Amy was a lip reader and had no sign language interpreter. In situations in which the teacher's back was to the class or Amy's peers were talking, she could not always read their lips and could not get the same information as the rest of the class. At her annual review, Amy's parents requested a sign language interpreter. The school district refused. Amy's parents took this matter up through various levels of hearing, court involvement, and eventually to the U.S. Supreme Court. The U.S. Supreme Court ruled that Amy did not require a sign language interpreter because she was making progress in the general education setting. In effect, they said that Amy was doing just fine. More specifically, they made the following distinctions:

> "... the requirement that a State provide specialized educational services ... generates no additional requirement that the services so provided by sufficient to maximize each child's potential."
>
> "... the furnishing of every special service necessary to maximize each handicapped child's potential is, we think, further than Congress intended it to go."
>
> The District Court found that the "evidence firmly establishes that Amy is receiving 'adequate' education, since she performs better than the average child in her class and is advancing easily from grade to grade."

This decision is grounded in the premise that the provision of a FAPE does not equate to an obligation to provide the best education or an education that maximizes the potential of the student. It went so far as to describe the legal requirement for providing an appropriate education as ensuring a "basic floor of opportunity." Unlike the Army motto of "Be All That You Can Be," the standard for public education is much less. It is adequate. It is just enough to level the playing field, nothing more.

Subsequent cases have underscored the Rowley decision by giving us additional language to define the idea of what constitutes (and what does not constitute) a FAPE. Most notable is the case that compares the delivery of an education to two cars—a Cadillac and a Chevy. The court, in *Doe v. Board of Education of Tullahoma City Schools*, 9 F.3d 455, 458 (6th Cir. 1993), cert. denied, 511 U.S. 1108, 114 S.Ct. 2104, 128 L.Ed.2d 665 (1994), described it in the following way:

> The Act requires that the Tullahoma schools provide the educational equivalent of a serviceable Chevrolet to every handicapped student. Appellant, however, demands that the Tullahoma school system

> provide a Cadillac solely for appellant's use. WE suspect that the Chevrolet offered to appellant is in fact a much nicer model than that offered to the average Tullahoma student. Be that as it may, we hold that the Board is not required to provide a Cadillac, and that the proposed IEP is reasonably calculated to provide educational benefits to appellant, and is therefore in compliance with the requirements of the IDEA.

The Cadillac versus Chevy analogy is likely to be a memorable distinction, as it gives an understandable and visual example of luxury versus simplicity. That is not to say however, that a FAPE need not be effective. It clearly must be able to get the job done. Other courts have highlighted this concept by stating the following:

> "The objective of [Rowley's 'basic floor of opportunity'] ... is the achievement of effective results—demonstrable improvement in the educational and personal skills identified as special needs—as a consequence of implementing the proposed IEP." *Town of Burlington v. Dep't of Educ. for Mass.*, 555 IDELR 526 (1st Cir. 1984).
>
> "This educational benefit 'cannot be a mere modicum of de minimus' but 'must be meaningful' and 'likely to produce progress.'" *Adam J. v. Keller Indep. Sch. Dist.*, 39 IDELR 1 (5th Cir. 2003).
>
> The IDEA "calls for more than a trivial educational benefit.... Congress intended to afford children with special needs an education that would confer meaningful benefit." *Polk v. Central Susquehanna Intermediate Unit No. 16*, 441 IDELR 130 (3rd Cir. 1988).

So you can see that although the term *FAPE* seems to be simple based on face value, it is actually full of complexities. It is at the heart of almost every special education conflict because of the differing views of what constitutes "adequate." As you might imagine, it is not uncommon for parents and schools to have diverse opinions on programming and levels of service that will be enough to produce progress. Some of the most common disagreements center around the parents' position that a higher level of service is needed, with the school arguing that what they are delivering is appropriate.

A frequent scenario I continue to see school districts grapple with is parents who are asking for more restrictive programming or a modified homework schedule for their child. They report that their child struggles at home, has extreme anxiety about school, may have emotional outbursts that last for hours, and needs intensive support to get homework done. They go on to report that they spend hours each night dealing with a combination of tantrums and homework. Conversely, the school has only experienced this student as someone who is unremarkable from their peers, with no problems either behaviorally or academically. From the school's vantage point, a FAPE is being delivered and there is no need to change anything. From the parent's vantage point, the situation is a crisis. This scenario plays out in many schools, especially with the increase of students grappling with a variety of mental illnesses. At the core of this conflict is the legal question of what is appropriate or what is a FAPE.

Compensatory Education

When a party believes that a FAPE has been denied, the result is often a request for compensatory education. Compensatory education seeks to compensate the student for programming or services that were denied entirely, compromised, or given inappropriately. For example, if your physical therapist leaves during the school year and you are unable to hire someone in her place, you know that you have an obligation to make up the time to those students who were to receive physical therapy. This type of compensatory service may take the form of paying for private providers or delivering services over the summer. There is no question that the students who have physical therapy in their IEP or 504 Plans require the service as a component of their FAPE. However, another example is when a parent seeks services from the school because they believe that the services given were inappropriate or ineffective. Perhaps test results come back that show little to no progress or the parent finds out that the teacher of service provider was not properly credentialed. These are situations in which the parent is likely to request that additional services be delivered to make up for that which was given inappropriately.

I represented a high school district in a compensatory education claim in which the school had placed the young man in a day school program for 9th and 10th grades. As his needs became more intense, he was moved to an out-of-state residential facility and remained there for the next several years. When it was time for him to exit the facility due to reaching the age of 22, his parents brought a compensatory education claim. They did so through the due process hearing procedures. They were pleased with the services that their son had received in the residential facility but argued that the school should have placed him there sooner than they did. Specifically, they were seeking compensatory education services for his 9th and 10th grade years. In effect, they wanted him to remain at the residential facility for another two years. The school was put in the position of proving that the services that they provided to him during 9th and 10th grades was appropriate, notwithstanding their ultimate decision to transfer him to a more restrictive setting. The school obtained a favorable ruling from the hearing officer and was not responsible for the two years of additional service. Unfortunately, the parents felt so ill-equipped to have their son home with them that they did not pick him up from the facility upon his release. He became a disabled adult ward of the state and entered another residential system.

We need to remember that the provision of a FAPE is not limited to an academic standard. Schools also have an obligation to address behavior and deliver services that result in the student being able to function appropriately at their level. After all, if the student does not have the social or interpersonal skills to get along with others or collaborate, their knowledge or skill levels will be secondary. Likewise, the functional skills of the student contribute to the provision of a FAPE. The ability of some students to learn self-help skills, hygiene, budgeting, and shopping may be important factors in deciding what constitutes the delivery of a FAPE. Case law is full of examples of situations where parents have filed for due process, declined their child's diploma, or requested compensatory educational services because they believed that the school did not deliver a FAPE with regard to adequately preparing their child for success in either the postsecondary or employment environments. The FAPE inquiry takes on many different forms and is worthy of your constant attention.

Least Restrictive Environment

To effectively provide a FAPE, the student must be in the appropriate environment in which he or she can have it delivered. This setting or least restrictive environment (LRE), according to the IDEA, would be as follows:

> "To the maximum extent appropriate, children with disabilities, . . . are educated with children who are nondisabled."
>
> Special classes, special schooling, or other removal . . . from the regular educational environment occurs only if the nature or severity of the disability is such that education in regular classes with the use of supplementary aids and services cannot be achieved satisfactorily. [34 CFR 300.114(a)(2)]

Although the intent of the law is certainly to provide students what they need in order to be successful, make progress, and receive a FAPE, it does so by taking somewhat of a minimalist approach. Specifically, the law only allows educators to provide what is necessary. It does not support extra service for the purpose of getting a head start. It does not authorize pulling the student into a small special education class where the ratio of staff to students is much lower because we think the student would benefit from it. Quite the contrary, the federal regulations specify that such type of exclusion should be done only when supports within the regular classes cannot be achieved satisfactorily. Your first consideration should be a general education class. Only when this option has been exhausted should you consider a more restrictive placement [*Letter to Cohen*, 25 IDELR 516 (OSEP 1996)].

Meeting the legal requirement to provide LRE doesn't mean that you cannot remove dangerous or disruptive students. See *School Bd. of Indep. Sch. Dist. No. 11 v. Renollett*, 45 IDELR 117 (8th Cir. 2006) and *Clyde K. v. Puyallup School District*, 21 IDELR 664 (9th Cir. 1994). Courts recognize that other students have a right to an education and that it needs to be provided in a safe environment. However, your staff should be prepared to list their efforts and strategies that were used before removing a student from their nondisabled peers.

In meeting with your team and deciding on placement, the IDEA specifies the following:

> The child's placement
>
> 1) Is determined at least annually; and
> 2) Is based on the child's IEP; and
> 3) Is as close as possible to the child's home;
>
> Unless the IEP of a child with a disability requires some other arrangement, the child is educated in the school that he or she would attend if nondisabled;
>
> In selecting LRE, give consideration to any potential harmful effect on the child or on the quality of services that he or she needs; and
>
> A child with a disability is not removed from education in age-appropriate regular classrooms solely because of needed modifications in the general education curriculum. (34 CFR 300.116)

Because a child's school experience also involves transportation, the Education Department has commented as follows: "It is assumed that most children with disabilities will receive the same transportation provided to nondisabled children, consistent with the LRE requirements in 34 CFR 300.114 through 34 CFR 300.120, unless the IEP determines otherwise" [71 Fed. Reg. 46, 576 (2006)].

Keep in mind that the LRE requirements also apply to nonacademic and extracurricular activities. The 2006 IDEA Part B regulations state:

> In providing or arranging for the provision of nonacademic and extracurricular services and activities, including meals, recess periods, . . . each public agency must ensure that each child

> with a disability participates with nondisabled children in the extracurricular services and activities to the maximum extent appropriate to the needs of that child.

A multitude of factors go into the determination of what constitutes the least restrictive environment for a student with a disability. An equal number of factors need to be monitored closely to ensure that the LRE concept is applied in different settings and throughout the school day. As you can see, the law requires staff to pay particular attention to any situation in which the student is excluded from nondisabled peers.

Discrimination

The prohibition against discrimination is a concept that is equally applicable under the IDEA as well as Section 504. The application of the FAPE and LRE requirements under IDEA should serve as an effective deterrent to either the categorical treatment of, or the exclusion of, students with disabilities. By providing a FAPE in the LRE, many discriminatory practices will be avoided. For a more thorough discussion of the components in the analysis of discrimination, refer to the section in Chapter 1.

Discussion Questions

The following are hypothetical situations for you and your team to consider and discuss. Important points and answers to each situation are outlined in Chapter 6.

Situation #1
Transfer Without Records

Jim transfers to your district without any school records. Jim's parents were silent as to his special education status. You later learn that Jim's IEP called for 40 minutes per week of speech services and 30 minutes per day in the resource room. Jim's parents now demand that you make up the time, in spite of the fact that they never let you know of the IEP services.

Are you denying FAPE if you don't make up the time?

Situation #2
Forgotten Parent Invite

Your new case manager forgets to invite the parents to the IEP meeting. They attend anyway.

Is this a violation of FAPE?

Situation #3
Incomplete IEP

Your new case manager forgets to write down 30 minutes of social work on the IEP and as a result, the student does not receive it for the entire school year.

Is this a violation of FAPE?

____

____

____

____

____

Situation #4
Inconsistent Data Collection

Jill's parents complain that after three years of occupational therapy, their daughter's skills have not progressed. After you review the IEP, you find that the goals have remained consistent and the data collection has been inconsistent. She has had the same therapist for the last three years.

What are the chances of a successful FAPE claim?

____

____

____

____

____

What are the chances of a successful compensatory claim?

____

____

____

Situation #5
Right To File A Complaint

Joe's parents request a Due Process Hearing based on the lack of "meaningful (academic) progress" that their son has made while receiving resource room assistance. The district argues that the parents were always in agreement with the implementation and services in the previous IEPs and that they have therefore given up their right to file a complaint now.

Will the district's argument be successful at hearing?

Will this FAPE claim be successful?

Situation #6
Mainstream Jane?

Jane's parents want her fully mainstreamed with her 5th grade classmates, despite the fact that she is functionally and cognitively at a prekindergarten level. The district believes that she is appropriately placed in the life skills class with peers who are at her ability level. This case will definitely go to Due Process if not resolved.

What is the LRE?

____

____

____

____

____

Situation #7
1:1 Aides

Your district is in a tough financial crisis. To cut down on the number of 1:1 aides that you employ, students who were previously given an aide for inclusion opportunities are now expected to either go alone or stay in the special education classroom. You have heard rumblings of a class action complaint by the parents.

Is this a violation of LRE?

____

____

____

____

____

Situation #8
Home School Curriculum

According to his IEP, Todd needs a life skills curriculum and a variety of related services. However, the special education classroom that offers the curriculum and services is located in a different school within the district. Todd's parents request that the curriculum and services be replicated in his home school and argue that it is the least restrictive environment.

What is the LRE?

Do you have to replicate programs?

Situation #9
Outside Placement

Mark is an emotionally disturbed student in your school. Staff members have exhausted their strategies and options for keeping him in the building and are now considering an outside placement. The parent agrees with this decision. You are confident that the cooperative program will meet Mark's needs but the parent wants a private therapeutic school. The parent's advocate has left a message for you to call her back.

What are your options?

____

____

____

____

____

____

____

What is the LRE?

____

____

____

____

____

____

____

See Chapter 6 for a legal analysis of these situations.

CHAPTER 3

The Elements of Section 504

"The whole is greater than the sum of its parts."

Aristotle

The starting point for understanding Section 504 is certainly the language of the law itself. In addition, regulatory guidance provides further clarification. But legal language is often subject to multiple interpretations, which may lead to inconsistent results. The application of the law is sometimes best understood through the real-life examples contained within case law. Another helpful resource is the response letters from the Office for Civil Rights to individuals who have made a formal inquiry. When OCR provides such guidance, the letters are published, cited, and referenced for future use. Utilizing these tools, we are better equipped to understand the meaning and application of Section 504 in the school environment.

Eligibility

The first consideration for eligibility under Section 504 is whether the student is "qualified." Qualification equates to being between the ages of 3 and 22 and a resident of the school system [34 CFR 104.3(k)(2)]. If these requirements are met, we move on to the meaning of disability as it applies to the student. A student is disabled within the meaning of Section 504 if he or she:

- Has a physical or mental impairment which substantially limits one or more major life activities,
- Has a record of such an impairment, or
- Is regarded as having such an impairment. [34 CFR 104.3(j)]

Physical or Mental Impairment

The first component contained within the definition of disability is the status of having a physical or mental impairment. Physical or mental impairment means:

> Any physiological disorder or condition, cosmetic disfigurement, or anatomical loss affecting one or more of the following body systems: neurological; musculoskeletal; special sense organs; respiratory, including speech organs; cardiovascular; reproductive; digestive genito-urinary; hemic and lymphatic; skin; and endocrine; or
>
> Any mental or psychological disorder, such as mental retardation, organic brain syndrome, emotional or mental illness, and specific learning disabilities. [34 CFR 104.3(j)(2)(i)]

It should be noted that this regulatory language is not exhaustive. Other diseases and conditions may also qualify as a physical or mental impairment.

Nothing in either Section 504 or its regulations expressly states that a disability must be permanent [*Letter to Rahall*, 21 IDELR 575 (OCR 1994)]. If an impairment is temporary but results in a substantial limitation for an extended period of time, that impairment is likely to qualify as a disability. If an impairment is episodic or in remission, it may qualify if it would substantially limit a major life activity when active. Guidance from OCR, entitled *Questions and Answers on the ADA Amendments Act of 2008 for Students with Disabilities Attending Public Elementary and Secondary Schools* (Q & A), addressed the issue of impairments as follows:

> In most cases, application of these rules should quickly shift the inquiry away from the question whether a student has a disability (and thus is protected by the ADA and Section 504) and toward the school district's actions and obligations to ensure equal education opportunities. While there are no per se disabilities under Section 504 and Title II, the nature of many impairments is such that in virtually every case, a determination in favor of disability will be made [emphasis added]. Thus, for example, a school district should not need or require extensive documentation or analysis to determine that a child with diabetes, epilepsy, bipolar disorder, or autism has a disability under Section 504 and Title II.

With this guidance in mind, erring on the side of a finding that supports the existence of an impairment is consistent with OCR's position.

Substantial Limitation

If your team has determined that a student has a physical or mental impairment, the next inquiry is it substantially limits a major life activity. The existence of an impairment, even in the form of a medical diagnosis, does not equate to the student being substantially limited. Many individuals have impairments but are not substantially limited. Students often learn compensatory skills and strategies to mask their challenges. In those cases in which the student may have an impairment but not be substantially limited in a major life activity, eligibility under Section 504 is not appropriate.

Unfortunately, Section 504 regulations do not define the term "substantial limits." The decision of whether a substantial limitation in a major life activity applies for a student should be made on a case-by-case basis [*Letter to McKethan*, 23 IDELR 504 (OCR 1995)]. When the ADA was originally enacted, the standard for substantial limitation was described as follows: "the individual's important life activities are restricted as to the conditions, manner, or duration under which they can be performed in the comparison to most people" [Rep. No. 101-116, at 23 (1989), and *Congressional Record* (Sept. 16, 2008), p. S8842]. In addition, the Equal Employment Opportunity Commission (EEOC) uses the definition of "substantial limits" as follows:

> Unable to perform a major life activity that the average person in the general population can perform; or
>
> Significantly restricted as to the condition, manner, or duration under which an individual can perform a major life activity as compared to the condition, manner, or duration under which the average person in the general population can perform that same major life activity. [29 CFR 1630.2(j)]

Initially, OCR interpreted substantial limitation to require an important and material limitation [*Pinellas County (FL) Sch. Dist.*, 20 IDELR 561 (OCR 1993)]. However, in 2008 the Americans with Disabilities Act Amendment Act (ADAAA) broadened the scope of the term by specifically stating, "An impairment need not prevent or severely or significantly restrict a major life activity to be considered substantially limiting" [42 USC §12102]. This language seems to expand the boundaries of what constitutes a substantial limitation.

Mitigating Measures

The concept of mitigating measures and how this plays into Section 504 eligibility has undergone some change. Initially, the "ameliorative effects of mitigating measures" were considered in the determination for eligibility. For example, a student who had severe allergies might have been brought to the team for their consideration but because of the "ameliorative effects" of the student receiving his allergy shots (otherwise known as the "mitigating measures"), the student did not qualify as an individual with a disability. Effective January 1, 2009, the ADAAA removed that language and stated that teams may not consider the ameliorative effects of mitigating measures. Using the previous example, the student with allergies would qualify as a student with a disability if, without receiving the shots, he would be substantially limited in a major life activity. Effectively, this language change does not penalize students from taking their medications and receiving treatment for their impairments.

Mitigating measures include things like medications, medical supplies, equipment or appliances, low-vision devices (which exclude ordinary eyeglasses or contact lenses), prosthetic devices, assistive technology, hearing aids and cochlear implants or other implantable hearing devices, mobility devices, oxygen therapy equipment and supplies, reasonable accommodations or auxiliary aids or services, or learned behavioral or adaptive neurological modifications that a person may use to eliminate or reduce the effects of an impairment. The team can qualify them as disabled if, without such measures, they would be substantially limited in a major life activity.

The exception to this language is that the team can consider the ameliorative effects of ordinary eyeglasses or contact lenses.

Major Life Activity

If the Section 504 team finds that the student has a physical or mental impairment that substantially limits him or her, the next step is to identify the major life activity that is affected. The Section 504 regulations have a non-exhaustive list of major life activities that include functions such as caring for one's self, preforming manual tasks, walking, seeing, hearing, speaking, breathing, learning, and working [34 CFR 104.3(j)(2)(ii)]. The ADAAA provided additional examples of major life activities that include:

- eating
- reading
- sleeping
- concentrating
- standing
- thinking
- walking
- communicating
- lifting
- speaking
- bending

Major bodily functions are also considered under the category of major life activities and include functions of the immune system, normal cell growth, digestive, bowel, bladder, neurological, brain, respiratory, circulatory, endocrine, and reproductive functions (42 USC §12102). Neither list is meant to be exhaustive, so the list can expand as necessary.

One of the purposes in giving so many examples of what may qualify as a major life activity is that school staff frequently needs to be reminded that learning is not the only consideration for a major life activity. Learning is but one of the major life activities that can be affected by a student's impairment. For example, a student who has diabetes is substantially limited in the area of endocrine function. A student with asthma is substantially limited in the area of breathing. A student with cancer is substantially limited in the area of normal cell growth.

After determining that the student has an impairment that substantially limits a major life activity, the next step is to evaluate the student to determine whether that student needs special education, related services, accommodations, or modifications in the school environment. The evaluation process and development of a Section 504 Plan will be outlined in Chapter 4.

Has a Record of Such an Impairment

The term "has a record of such an impairment" means has a history of or has been misclassified as having, a mental or physical impairment that substantially limits one or more major life activities [34 CFR §104.3(j)(2)(iii)]. An example of this situation would be student who has been cured of, or who no longer has, their impairment but who nevertheless receives follow-up or monitoring appointments with a health care provider.

The status of having a "record of" is insufficient, by itself, for any entitlement to treatment such as FAPE or reasonable accommodations. However, if a decision is made or an action is completed that has a discriminatory effect and that decision or action was based on the person's status as having a "record of" an impairment, Section 504 is designed to protect that type of individual.

Is Regarded as Having Such an Impairment

The term "is regarded as having an impairment" means:

> Has a physical or mental impairment that does not substantially limit major life activities but that is treated by a recipient as constituting such a limitation;
>
> Has a physical or mental impairment that substantially limits major life activities only as a result of the attitudes of others toward such impairment; or
>
> Has none of the impairments defined . . . but is treated by a recipient as having such impairment. [34 CFR §104.3(j)(2)(iv)]

The "regarded as" language can be confusing because it is premised on the perception and treatment from others. For example, if school staff mistakenly believes that a student has an impairment and take actions based on that mistaken belief, the action may constitute discrimination. Section 504 protects individuals from discrimination even if they are mistaken for someone who has an actual impairment.

Students who are "regarded as" having an impairment does not automatically qualify for a Section 504 Plan, complete with modifications and accommodations. They are, however, protected from discrimination that could include protection from retaliation and harassment.

Temporary Impairments

Generally, temporary impairments do not qualify for eligibility under Section 504. The exception to this rule is that if the impairment results in a substantial limitation of one or more major life activities for an extended period of time, it qualifies for eligibility. Further clarification on what the term "extended period" means can be found in the Amendments Act §4(a) (codified as amended at 42 USC §12102) as having an actual or expected duration of six months or less. The other consideration that must be taken into account, on a case-by-case basis, is the extent to which the temporary impairment limits a major life activity. If the impairment can be categorized as minor, it does not meet the standard for eligibility. Thus, your school teams will need to examine both the duration of the temporary impairment as well as the severity.

A situation that many schools are facing today is the treatment of students who have suffered a concussion. In many cases, the duration of the impairment is uncertain. The modifications and accommodations required may be extensive (e.g., limited reading, no computer monitor exposure, P.E. restrictions, etc.). In many cases, the 504 team has decided that both eligibility and a formal 504 Plan are warranted due to the indeterminate nature of this condition.

Contrast the concussion example to the case of *James A. Garfield (OH) Local School District,* 52 IDELR 142 (OCR 2009), in which the parent of a student with a broken foot had requested a tutor, early release from class and someone to carry her son's books. OCR determined that the injury was not substantially limiting since its duration was just for three months.

The lack of 504 eligibility or a formal 504 Plan does not mean that staff will not exercise best practice measures to ensure that the student will be successful; it simply means that the process and procedures involved in eligibility and 504 Plan development are unnecessary.

Complex Eligibility

Several conditions can be categorized as areas of complex eligibility when examining whether a student qualifies for the protections under Section 504. The reason for them being categorized as complex is due to changes in the wording/coverage under the law or the complexity of the condition itself. The conditions that will be discussed will be alcoholism, drug addiction, and attention-deficit disorder (ADD). Due to changes in the law specifically regarding alcoholism and drug addiction, the historical background and position on these impairments will be outlined.

Applicable Laws and Guidance

Before discussing the changes in the wording and positions contained within the legal guidance on alcoholism and drug addiction, it is helpful to understand the timelines of the law. In 1973, the Rehabilitation Act was passed, with Section 504 being just one of the sections of this law.

In 1990, the Americans with Disabilities Act (ADA) was passed. The language in the ADA was similar, if not identical, in many areas to the language in Section 504. Although the ADA was seen as groundbreaking legislation in a number of venues, schools had been addressing the needs of students with disabilities for a number of years. In 2008, the ADA Amendments Act of 2008 (ADAA) (Public Law 110-325) was passed. It became effective on January 1, 2009. The language of the ADAA was necessary to clarify some issues that the private sector was having regarding eligibility for ADA protections. One of the larger issues was that employers were denying their disabled employees coverage under the ADA by asserting that they were not "substantially limited." These cases were going to court, several even making it to the Supreme Court, with the courts siding on the behalf of employers. Therefore, it was extremely difficult for a disabled individual to get qualified under the ADA and to obtain the accommodations needed.

In the ADAA, Congress articulated its displeasure over the courts' rulings by stating:

> While Congress expected that the definition of a disability under the ADA would be interpreted consistently with how courts had applied the definition of a handicapped individual under the Rehabilitation Act of 1973, that expectation has not been fulfilled.

The ADAA went on to provide more guidance on the definition of a disability and made the rather sweeping statement that,

> The definition of disability in this Act shall be construed in favor of broad coverage of individuals under this Act, to the maximum extent permitted by the terms of this Act. [Sec. 3(4)(A)]

The message was clear; coverage for disabled individuals was to be expanded to allow them a level playing field.

With this legal backdrop in mind, we turn to the conditions of alcoholism and drug addiction as they pertain to Section 504 eligibility.

Alcoholism and Drug Use

Section 504 and Regulatory Language

The comments to the Section 504 regulations provide that "drug addiction and alcoholism are physical or mental impairments within the meaning of Section 7(6) of the Rehabilitation Act of 1973 and that drug addicts and alcoholics are therefore [disabled] for purposes of Section 504 if their impairment substantially limits one of their major life activities" [34 CFR Part 104, Appendix A (4)]. The comments go on to discuss that despite consensus that these conditions qualify as diseases, "there is disagreement as to whether they are primarily mental or physical."

Within the employment context, an alcoholic or drug addict may not be denied services or disqualified from employment based solely on their condition. If however, the individual cannot perform the job in a satisfactory manner, cannot comply with the rules of the organization, or cannot exhibit behavior that is appropriate to the situation, then the protections under Section 504 do not apply. Borrowing language from the Americans with Disabilities Act, the individual must be able to perform the "essential functions of the job."

The Americans with Disabilities Act

When the Americans with Disabilities Act was passed in 1990, it narrowed the definition of an individual with a handicap. Specifically, it excluded persons ". . . currently engaging in the illegal use of drugs." Thereafter, OCR went on to define "current illegal use of drugs" as "illegal use of drugs that occurred recently enough to justify a reasonable belief that a person's drug use is current or that continuing use is a real and ongoing problem" [*OCR Senior Staff Memorandum,* 19 IDELR 859 (OCR 1992)]. This clarification contains no reference to a requirement that the drug use be an addiction. Therefore, the "recreational" use of illegal drugs may also fall into this definition.

This new ADA language had the effect of amending the 504 definition regarding the current use of illegal drugs. Therefore, a student engaged in the illegal use of drugs is not a "qualified individual with a disability" and not eligible for protections under the law.

Alcohol Use

The ADA was silent, and therefore did not exclude, those who were alcoholics or engaged in alcohol use. Subsequent case law established that a student with alcoholism may qualify under Section 504 for protections if the impairment substantially limited one or more major life activities. See *Pinellas County (FL) Sch. Dist.,* 20 IDELR 561 (OCR 1993).

Rehabilitation

With respect to individuals who are in recovery or participating in a drug rehabilitation program, the protections of both 504 and the ADA apply. Specifically, it applies to a student who:

- Has successfully completed a supervised drug rehabilitation program and is no longer engaging in the illegal use of drugs, or has otherwise been rehabilitated successfully and is no longer engaging in such use;
- Is participating in a supervised rehabilitation program and is no longer engaging in such use; or
- Is erroneously regarded as engaging in such use, but is not engaging in such use. [29 USC 705(20)(c)(ii)]

Discipline

With regard to the discipline of students with these conditions, we have the following federal guidance on disciplinary action:

> For purposes of programs and activities providing educational services, local educational agencies may take disciplinary action pertaining to the use of possession of illegal drugs or alcohol against any student who is an individual with a disability and who currently is engaging in the illegal use of drugs or in the use of alcohol to the same extent that such disciplinary action is taken against students who are not individuals with disabilities. Furthermore, the due process procedures. . .shall not apply to such disciplinary actions. [29 USC 705 (20)(C)(iv)]

In addition, OCR has given the following guidance:

> Both the ADA and the amended Section 504 also allow school districts to take disciplinary action pertaining to the use of possession of illegal drugs against any student with a disability who is currently engaging in the illegal use of drugs to the same extent that such disciplinary action is taken against nondisabled students. [*Letter to Zirkel*, 22 IDELR 667 (OCR 1995)]

The Americans with Disabilities Amendment Act

The ADAA did not make any changes to the definition of a "qualified individual with a disability." As such, the definitions and protections for individuals under the ADA were maintained.

Attention-Deficit/Hyperactivity Disorder (ADHD)

One of the most frequent questions from school staff centers around the eligibility of the ADHD student for either IDEA or Section 504 services. Consider the following example:

> Homer and Bart are students in your class, each having a doctor's note identifying them as individuals with ADHD. Homer is on medication and is an exemplary student. You believe Bart may be the next poster child for ADHD—he struggles with all aspects of school and attention issues. You have received requests from both sets of parents for 504 Plans.

In this case, each student is affected by their ADHD in different ways. They will therefore receive treatment that is individualized to their needs. For Homer, a Section 504 Plan initially seems unnecessary, as his medication is effective and he is unremarkable from his peers. Remember however, that you cannot consider the ameliorative effects of medication. So the most prudent course of action is to evaluate Homer and get more information on what type of student he is when not taking the medication. According to the ADAA, Homer is definitely not precluded from a 504 evaluation just because he is on medication. He can also qualify as an individual with a disability.

However, this does not equate to an automatic 504 Plan. The team needs to consider whether, because of his substantial limitation from his ADHD, he requires special education or related services. 34 CFR 104.3(l), 104.33 If he does not require these services, there is no need to develop a 504 Plan. He would be afforded the protections of the law as they relate to freedom from discrimination but not a 504 Plan.

For Bart, the need for support is apparent. Depending on the level of need, the team may wish to consider Bart's eligibility under IDEA. One of the key factors in this decision is whether Bart needs more of an instructional approach to support him or whether he needs more peripheral assistance. Notwithstanding that a Section 504 Plan offers a continuum of services, there should be some thought to IDEA eligibility when the disability requires more of an instructional approach. Let's take this concept into the next example:

Case Example : ADHD

Johnny

Johnny has ADHD. In order to function successfully in the school environment, he needs someone to do a "check in" with him in the morning after he gets off the school bus. Checking to make sure that he is ready for the day includes looking through his backpack for the required books, homework, and assignment notebook. It also requires a brief conversation with Johnny to ensure that he is emotionally ready for the day. At the end of the school day, this same type of check is necessary. No other services are required.

Jill also has ADHD. Her attention is so compromised that she misses many of the skills taught in her math class. In order to keep up with the class, she requires an extra period of math for reinforcement.

Johnny's situation is best addressed with a Section 504 Plan. His support could be implemented by a variety of people including a resource room teacher, guidance counselor, paraprofessional, or social worker. Jill's situation is more complex and because it requires an instructional approach, the team may want to consider IDEA eligibility. In that case, the disability category applicable would be Other Health Impaired (OHI) because her "strength, alertness, or vitality" is limited and adversely affects her educational performance [34 CFR 300.8(c)(9), Letter to Cohen, 20 IDELR 73 (OSEP 1993)].

Medical Documentation

Requiring parents to supply medical documentation of a student's ADHD status can have financial implications for the school. Specifically, the Office for Civil Rights said, in *OCR Response to Veir*, 20 IDELR 864 (1993), that a district cannot require the parent to provide a medical statement if they suspect that the student has a disability and is eligible under Section 504. If the district believes that a medical assessment is necessary in order to conduct an appropriate evaluation, the district must "ensure that the child receives this assessment at no cost to the parents." Therefore, requiring parents to supply medical documentation of their child's disability may also obligate the school to fund it. This is the free concept as contained within the FAPE acronym.

In the case of *Broward County (FL) School District,* 58 IDELR 292 (OCR 2012), the school district had a policy of requiring a medical diagnosis (on letterhead) of a student's disability before initiating the RTI process that led into the 504 eligibility determination process. OCR responded to the parent's complaint and ordered that the school remedy the situation so that there was no cost to the parent.

Many parents have medical documentation that they are willing to share. OCR's guidance does not prohibit the school from taking what is offered and considering it in the evaluation process. There should be clarity with the parents that the medical documentation that they have volunteered is appreciated but not required.

Discussion Questions

The following are hypothetical situations for you and your team to consider and discuss. Important points and answers to each situation are outlined in Chapter 6.

Situation #1
Diabetes

Lisa is a student with diabetes. She was recently diagnosed, and her condition is unstable. She frequently misses class to eat her snack, check her blood sugar, and occasionally adjust her insulin dosage.

Is Lisa eligible under Section 504?

____

____

____

____

____

Situation #2
ADHD

Tim is a student with ADHD. He takes a time-released medication at home and never requires medical supervision during the school day. Until recently, the school never knew of Tim's ADHD status. Tim's parents recently came to the school district and requested a Section 504 Plan. They said it will assist him in getting a better score on his upcoming ACT. As you review Tim's file, including his academic and disciplinary history, you see nothing remarkable. In fact, Tim is an exemplary student with average to above-average grades.

Is Tim eligible under Section 504?

Situation #3
Sexuality

Joseph has just "come out" with his sexuality. In sharing this information with his classmates, he is taunted mercilessly. His lawyer contacts the district and alleges a possible suit based on harassment and discrimination.

Is Joseph eligible under Section 504?

If not, what type of case is this and what is your plan of action?

Situation #4
Sports Injury

Rebecca has a cheerleading injury that requires her to have surgery and pins in her leg. She will be on crutches for at least 7 months. Teachers have been accommodating and have allowed Rebecca an alternate passing period, a locker "buddy," and an extra set of books for home. Rebecca's mother comes into the school and requests a Section 504 Plan.

What is your response?

____

____

____

____

____

Situation #5
Peanut Allergy

Garrett is a recent transfer student in the first grade. As the district's 504 coordinator, you are contacted by Garrett's mother who insists on a meeting to set up a 504 Plan for her son. She brings in medical documentation of Garrett's fatal peanut allergy. She has a laundry list of classroom accommodations and environmental changes that will have to be made in order for Garrett to be safe in the school environment.

Is Garrett eligible under Section 504?

____

____

____

____

____

Situation #6
AIDS

As the building administrator, you learn of a student's recent AIDS diagnosis. The student is not currently compromised by his condition. You meet with the parent to discuss a possible 504 Plan but the parent tells you that she does not want other staff to know of her son's condition for confidentiality reasons. She refuses to participate in the development of a 504 Plan and says she will take legal action if you intend on pursuing it.

Do you pursue it in the interest of school liability?

____

____

____

____

____

Situation #7
Accommodating A Parent With Disabilities

A parent with disabilities within the district calls and informs you that she plans on attending her son's holiday classroom performance this evening but will need preferential seating and a sign language interpreter. She wishes to be seated in one of the first two rows. The sign language interpreter charges a minimum of $500 due to the late notice, in addition to the hourly rate.

Do you have to make the requested accommodations?

____

____

____

____

____

See Chapter 6 for a legal analysis of these situations.

CHAPTER 4

Development of the Section 504 Plan

"A plan is only as good as those who see it through"

Anonymous

FOLLOWING SECTION 504: PUBLIC VS. PRIVATE SCHOOLS

Section 504 directly addresses the question of whether your school, program, or activity is required to adhere to its requirements. Specifically it applies to "preschool, elementary, secondary, and adult education programs and activities that receive or benefit from Federal financial assistance." It is safe to say that all public schools receive some sort of federal financial assistance, so the obligations within Section 504 will apply to them.

Section 504 may also apply to private institutions due to its language that states, "... recipients that operate, or that receive or benefit from Federal financial assistance for the operation of, such programs or activities" (34 CFR104.31). Therefore, if a private school or program is directly receiving or benefiting from federal financial assistance, they are also responsible for following the mandates contained within Section 504.

CHILD FIND

The child find obligation is appropriately named: you are to find those children who you believe may have a disability. This obligation also extends to taking appropriate steps to notify the disabled person and their parents or guardians of your obligation (34 CFR 104.32). In many cases, schools tend to rely on parents to initiate the evaluation process. It is important to remember that the child find responsibility belongs to the school, not the parent. Take for example the case of *Isle of Wight County (VA) Public Schools*, 56 IDELR 111 (OCR 2010), in which the student was diabetic and had unpredictable fluctuations in his blood sugar levels. The student was expelled for a verbal threat and the parents filed a complaint with OCR citing a failure to evaluate the student under Section 504. OCR responded to the school as follows,

"... it is not the parent's responsibility, but rather the Division's to identify and evaluate any student who needs or is believed to need special education or related services because of disability."

In determining whether your school is complying with the child find obligation, you may wish to review your internal process of identifying students who are struggling behaviorally, academically, or medically. You may also want to review your parent–student handbook or other district notices to ensure that they contain a reference to eligibility under Section 504.

Individual Health Care Plans

OCR has found child find violations in several cases dealing with districts choosing to implement individual health care plans instead of Section 504 Plans. In *Tyler (TX) Independent School District, 56 IDELR 24* (OCR 2010), the district addressed the needs of students with diabetes, and in *Dracut (MA) Public Schools*, 110 LRP 48748 (OCR 2010), the district addressed the needs of a student with a peanut allergy. In both cases, the districts chose to use an individual health care plan instead of a Section 504 Plan. In both cases, OCR found that the districts had violated their child find requirement under Section 504.

An individual health care plan is actually a term coined in education but not in the law. As such, no procedural safeguards or requirements exist that must be followed. OCR is not in favor of them when a Section 504 Plan could be implemented.

From a liability standpoint, consider the loose nature of an individual health care plan; usually the school nurse is the person responsible for its implementation and follow-through measures. If the nurse happens to make an error, safeguards are not usually present. Contrast this scenario with a Section 504 Plan with its team effort, scheduled meetings for purposes of updates and progress, and a mechanism for parents to use if they are dissatisfied with either the implementation or progress under the plan. Taken as a whole, the Section 504 Plan is legally a much "safer" document and affords parents' rights that are not present in the health care plan.

Initial Evaluation

If an evaluation of a student is warranted, parental consent is needed before the team can commence the evaluation process [*Letter to Durheim*, 27 IDELR 380 (OCR 1997); see also *OCR Senior Staff Memorandum*, 19 IDELR 892 (OCR 1992)].

One of the most neglected requirements of Section 504 is the requirement to conduct an eligibility evaluation of the student. Many times, schools are not aware of the process for eligibility or that the team may possibly find a student ineligible under 504. No absolute right to an evaluation is provided. A district can refuse a parental request for an evaluation but upon doing so, the district must make available the process to appeal the decision [*OCR Response to Mentink,* 19 IDELR 1127(1993)].

Too often, schools accept the parent's report or doctor's script and automatically go forward with the development of a 504 Plan. However, a medical diagnosis alone does not automatically entitle a student to services under Section 504. [See *Frequently Asked Questions About Section 504 and the Education of Children with Disabilities,* 111 LRP 76408 (OCR 2011).] Section 504 requires that schools conduct an evaluation of students "who, because of handicap, need or are believed to need special education or related services" [34 CFR 104.35(a)].

The evaluation can consist of testing as well as sources of information that already exist in the school setting. Existing sources include grades, attendance records, disciplinary referrals, health information, teacher comments, standardized test scores, language surveys, and parent information. If testing is done, Section 504 requires that they are validated for the specific purpose for which they are used and are administered by trained personnel [34 CFR 104.35(b)(1)]. Appendix A to Section 504 explains that the school is to draw from "a variety of sources in the evaluation process so that the possibility of error in classification is minimized."

Section 504 contains no language that establishes a timeline for completion of an evaluation for eligibility. However, OCR has ruled in a number of cases that failure to conduct an evaluation within a reasonable period after referral violates Section 504 when it denies an eligible student an appropriate education. Examples of delays between referral and evaluation that have been found to be inappropriate range from 5–18 months. [See, e.g., *La Honda-Pescadero (Calif.) Unified Sch. Dist.*, 20 IDELR 833 (OCR 1993), *Community High Sch. Dist. 155 (IL),* 51 IDELR 228(OCR 2008).]

Once the evaluation is completed, the data are reviewed by a multi-disciplinary team for placement purposes. The team includes people who are knowledgeable about the child, the meaning of the evaluation data, and the placement options [34 CFR 104.35(c)(3)]. Although parents are not specifically named as members of the group, they should be invited to participate. The purpose of the team is to determine eligibility and to develop, if appropriate, the 504 Plan within the least restrictive environment (34 CFR 104.34).

The Section 504 Plan

Once the team has determined eligibility under Section 504, they should turn their attention to the development of a 504 Plan. The starting point for any

504 Plan is an understanding of the disability and how it affects the major life activity of the student. Remember, learning is not the only major life activity under consideration. The 504 Plan should outline how the disability impacts the student in the school environment. After the team has outlined the impact, they turn to brainstorming ways to "level the playing field."

FAPE

Under Section 504, students are entitled to a free, appropriate public education (34 CFR 104.33). For every student, this appropriate public education looks different. It is important to note that students are not limited as to what they can receive under a Section 504 Plan. The plan is not limited to accommodations and modifications in the general education setting. Students can receive their education in regular classes with the use of supplementary services or special education and related services. A FAPE can even take the form of an alternative placement or residential facility [34 CFR 104 Appendix A (23)].

OCR has differentiated between the school and employment environments and has given guidance on the topic of FAPE as it relates to the concept of reasonable accommodation. Under the ADA in the employment context, the employer who is faced with a request from a disabled employee for accommodations has the option to decide that such accommodations are not reasonable. Many reasons can be given for a denial, such as cost, inconvenience, and undue hardship. However, in the school environment, OCR has stated as follows:

> The key question ... is whether OCR reads into the Section 504 regulatory requirement for a free appropriate public education (FAPE) a "reasonable accommodation" standard, or other similar limitation. The clear and unequivocal answer to that is no. [*Letter to Zirkel*, 20 IDELR 134 (OCR 1993)]

This bold message from OCR is clear that schools must put into place whatever accommodations, modifications, services, or placement options are necessary to provide a FAPE to a disabled student under Section 504. Discussion of cost, inconvenience, hardship or willingness is irrelevant. Whatever it takes must be done.

The FAPE is designed to be given in the LRE, specifically, the environment that affords the disabled student the maximum exposure to nondisabled peers. However, in some situations the behavior of the disabled student is disruptive to the learning of others. In these cases, the law does not support a general education placement and allows for a more restrictive environment to be chosen [34 CFR 104 Appendix A(24)].

Accommodations vs. Modifications

In order to communicate clearly to parents about the services that will be provided to their child, it is important to distinguish between an accommodation and a modification. An accommodation is a change in the format or environment. As an example, sending a student to the resource room to take a test is an accommodation. Enlarging the font size on curricular material is an accommodation. The key is that the learning standard has not changed; the disabled student is responsible for learning the same material as nondisabled peers.

A modification is a change in the content. As an example, giving a child a multiple choice test when all the other students have to complete a fill in the blank test would be a modification. After all, the skill of word recognition in multiple choice is far easier than the skill of word recall in a fill in the blank test. Another example would be decreasing the spelling words in a test from 20 words to 10 words. The disabled student is not being held responsible for the same amount of words as nondisabled peers. The expectation for learning and the skill level is different for the disabled student when implementing a modification.

It is important to communicate with both parents and team members about the accommodations and modifications contained within the 504 Plan. If significant modifications are planned, it is critical that parents are able to understand the efforts that are necessary in order for the student to benefit from the instructional setting. Team members, especially those who were not present at the conference, also need to appreciate their role in facilitating the requirements of the plan. When parties have a common understanding of the extent to which the student needs to be supported and the measures that need to be taken, the chances of conflict at a later date are greatly diminished.

Reevaluation

Section 504 regulations only require that reevaluations occur periodically. In determining how to interpret this requirement, the language goes on to state that compliance with the IDEA is one means of compliance with Section 504. Therefore, mirroring the three-year reevaluation cycle under the IDEA will result in Section 504 compliance.

A reevaluation is also necessary when a school plans to implement a significant change of placement. OCR would consider the following to be significant changes in placement:

Transferring a student from one program to another

Terminating services

Excluding a student from the educational program for more than 10 school days

OCR has ruled that parental consent is not needed for the reevaluation process [*Letter to Durheim*, 27 IDELR 380 (OCR 1997); see also *OCR Senior Staff Memorandum*, 19 IDELR 892 (OCR 1992)].

Procedural Safeguards

Section 504 mandates that schools establish and implement procedural safeguards with respect to their efforts in identification, evaluation, or educational placement of students who have disabilities or who are suspected of having a disability. The procedural safeguards must address the areas of notice, an opportunity for parents or guardians of the person to examine relevant records, an impartial hearing with an opportunity for participation by the person's parents or guardians, representation by counsel, and a review procedure (34 CFR 104.36). To make these requirements manageable, the regulations go on to say that compliance with the procedural safeguards of the IDEA is one means of meeting the Section 504 procedural safeguards requirement (34 CFR 104.36).

OCR, as the enforcing entity for Section 504, takes a careful look at procedural compliance. However, they are not typically as focused on individual cases and their outcomes as long as the procedural safeguards have been afforded. The Section 504 regulations contain this language in the appendix:

> It is not the intention of the Department, except in extraordinary circumstances, to review the result of individual placement and other educational decision, so long as the school district complies with the "process" requirements of this subpart. [34 CFR 104 Appendix A(21)]

Taking stock of procedural safeguards under the IDEA, and ensuring that they are identical to your Section 504 safeguards, is one way of preventing an oversight that can lead to costly conflict and litigation.

Notice

Section 504 requires that parents receive notice "with respect to actions regarding the identification, evaluation, or educational placement of persons, who because of handicap, need or are believed to need special education or related services" (34 CFR 104.36). The types of notice forms your school should have in place include the following:

1) Notice of Section 504 conferences
2) Notice of Section 504 evaluation and reevaluation decisions
3) Notice of Section 504 evaluation results and eligibility decisions

4) Notice of Section 504 programmatic decisions
5) Notice of any significant change in placement, including disciplinary removals beyond 10 days
6) Notice of termination of Section 504 services or eligibility
7) Notice of procedural safeguards

Even though Section 504 does not provide the detail of exactly what needs to be in the notices, OCR has given guidance that the notices should be specific enough to allow parents to decide whether they want to consent or decline the services or request due process [see, e.g., *Middleton-Cross Plains (WI) Area Sch. Dist.* 16 IDELR 763 (OCR 1990)].

OCR also requires a general nondiscrimination notice [see, e.g., *Ansonia (CT) Public Schools*, 56 IDELR (OCR 2010)]. This notice is to inform the public that as a recipient of federal funds, and in compliance with Section 504, the school does not discriminate on the basis of disability in its programs or activities.

Section 504 Coordinator

For districts that have 15 or more employees, Section 504 requires that at least one person is designated to coordinate its compliance efforts [34 CFR 104.7(a)]. Contained within the nondiscrimination notice should be the identity of the coordinator [34 CFR 104.8(a)]. Failure to identify the coordinator may be an actionable violation of Section 504 [*Garfield (NJ) School District*, 18 IDELR 545 (OCR 1991)]. Section 504 does not specify the credentials that the coordinator must have relative to performing the duties.

The ADA also has a requirement for an individual to be identified for purposes of coordinating efforts to comply with the ADA (28 CFR 35.107). No prohibition is made against the same person serving as both 504 and ADA coordinator. However, the law does not assume that identifying one person as a coordinator automatically requires that person to coordinate both laws.

Grievances and Hearings

The regulations to Section 504 require that if a school employs more than 15 employees, grievance procedures must be developed "for the prompt and equitable resolution of complaints" [34 CFR 104.7(b)]. These procedures must be available to parents, students, employees, and third parties [see, e.g., *Maine (ME) School Administrative District #13*, 55 IDELR 84 (OCR 2009)].

OCR has outlined the following components in their review of whether a board's grievance procedures are prompt and equitable:

1) Adequate, reliable, and impartial investigation of complaints, including the opportunity to present witnesses and other evidence;
2) Designated and reasonably prompt tie frames for the major stages of the complaint process;
3) Notice to the parties of the outcome of the complaint; and
4) An assurance that steps will be taken to promptly and effectively end the discrimination, prevent its recurrence and to remedy its effects. [*Ansonia (CT) Public Schools*, 56 IDELR (OCR 2010)]

In the case of *Ansonia* case, OCR found that the district failed on a number of levels in their 504 procedures. First, they found that the identified 504 compliance officers did not have an understanding of the obligations under Section 504. Second, they found that having those compliance officers serve as hearing officers to review decisions regarding the identification, evaluation, and placement of students with disabilities was inappropriate. Third, they found that the district did not notify their parents who fell in the "nation-origin minority group" of policies and procedures in a language other than English. Further, they failed to translate important policies and procedures into Spanish. OCR has given further guidance on the qualifications of hearing officers and has ruled that districts may not use their own employees as hearing officers or use employees of another district when a contractual arrangement is in place regarding servicing special needs students [*Leon County (FL) Sch. Dist.*, 50 IDELR 172 (OCR 2007); *Griffith (IN) Pub. Schs.*, 40 IDELR 105 (OCR 2003)].

OCR has reviewed many cases on the topic of grievance procedures and has made clear the importance of developing a comprehensive grievance procedure that is available to the parents and of implementing the procedures as published as well as ensuring that the compliance/coordinators have a good working knowledge of their responsibilities under the law. If the grievance process goes forward into a hearing mode, the hearing officer must also be knowledgeable about the law and be an impartial party. Employees, board members, and others with an interest in the district should be avoided. In this way, the process can be free from bias and the hearing officer can deliver decisions that are free from any partiality.

Discussion Questions

The following are hypothetical situations for you and your team to consider and discuss. Important points and answers to each situation are outlined in Chapter 6.

Situation #1
Teacher Accommodations

After the 504 coordinator reminds the high school English teacher of her responsibilities under the terms of a 504 Plan written for one of her students, the teacher requests a meeting with the coordinator and the president of the union. The teacher claims that implementation of the plan constitutes a change in working conditions and, quite frankly, she does not have the time or resources to make all of the required accommodations.

Can the teacher successfully argue this claim?

____

____

____

____

____

____

Situation #2
Anxiety Disorder

Mr. and Mrs. Baker present a doctor's script identifying their daughter as having an anxiety disorder. They request the immediate development of a 504 Plan with the accommodations of extended time on homework, excusal for late arrival, and social work services.

What is your response?

____

____

____

____

____

Situation #3
Transition to High School

The elementary school district has a practice of developing a large number of 504 Plans for students during their 8th grade school year so they will be supported as they go on to high school. The high school believes many of the plans are unnecessary.

What action should the high school take?

____

____

____

____

____

Situation #4

Transfer Student

A student transfers to your school with records that include an individual health care plan. The parent is pleased with the plan and expects it to be followed as written.

What do you do?

Situation #5

More Than 100 Accommodations

Mr. Simpson has recently been told that his daughter, Lisa, has diabetes. He comes to the school with the doctor's script as well as a three-page document listing more than 100 accommodations and modifications that he says will need to be implemented. He shares with you that the accommodations document was obtained from the Internet as something that needs to be in every 504 Plan for a diabetic.

How do you respond?

See Chapter 6 for a legal analysis of these situations.

CHAPTER 5

A Legal Comparison of IDEA and Section 504

"The highest result of education is tolerance."

Helen Keller

The similarities in the purpose, scope, and wording between the IDEA and Section 504, often cause confusion as to which law controls. It can also be confusing as to when an Individual Education Program (IEP) is appropriate and when a Section 504 Plan is appropriate. The legal components of both laws will be discussed with a focus on similarities and differences.

Types of Laws

The IDEA is a federal funding statute. It is designed to ensure that students with disabilities are afforded an appropriate education. It also provides financial funding to states in an effort to assist them in delivering needed services to students with disabilities.

Section 504 is a civil rights law that protects individuals with disabilities from discrimination in programs and activities that receive federal financial assistance from the U.S. Department of Education. No funding is associated with this law.

Eligibility

Under IDEA, eligibility is met when the student qualifies for one of thirteen federal categories of disabilities. The student must be adversely affected in their educational performance. An IEP document is then developed to outline the special education and related services that are needed to afford the student their right to a FAPE.

Section 504 covers individuals who have a physical or mental impairment that substantially limits a major life activity. It also protects from discrimination those individuals who have a history of the impairment or those who are regarded as having an impairment. Once eligible, a Section 504 Plan is developed to outline the services needed to deliver a FAPE.

Least Restrictive Environment

Under both IDEA and Section 504, the student is entitled to receive a FAPE in the least restrictive environment. This environment must be both appropriate to meet the student's needs as well as in a setting with maximum exposure to nondisabled peers. It does not automatically equate to a setting in the general education environment; the setting can be more restrictive as long as it is appropriate in meeting the student's needs.

The Team

Under the IDEA, specific individuals are identified as team members, including the parent. Terms outlining the attendance of team members are also provided.

Section 504 contains more general language and refers to, "a group of persons, including persons knowledgeable about the child" (34 CFR 104.35). Although parent participation is not specifically mentioned, it is considered best practice.

Reevaluation

Under the IDEA, a reevaluation must be done every three years to reestablish eligibility. This process can include formal testing, a records review, or both. A reevaluation is not required before graduation or aging out, but a summary of academic achievement and functional performance must be completed. Included in this documentation are recommendations on how to assist the student in meeting postsecondary goals.

Section 504 does not specify a timeline for reevaluation, only referring to the requirement to do so periodically. Compliance with the timeline under the IDEA is considered compliance under Section 504. A reevaluation is required before a significant change in placement. OCR has given guidance that parental consent is not necessary for reevaluations [*Letter to Durheim*, 27 IDELR 380 (OCR 1997)].

Manifestation Determination Review

Under both the IDEA and Section 504, a manifestation determination review (MDR) is required before taking action to expel the student or for a removal that constitutes a change of placement.

Revocation of Consent

Parents clearly have the right to revoke services under the IDEA (34 CFR 300.300). However, whether parents are allowed to revoke their child's IDEA services and then request/receive services for their child under Section 504 remains an issue of some conflict. In *Letter to McKethan*, 25 IDELR 295 (OCR 1996), OCR said that a rejection of the IDEA services served as a rejection of services under Section 504. Other cases have had similar rulings [*Lamkin v. Lone Jack C-6 Sch. Dist.*, 58 IDELR 197 (W.D. Mo. 2012)]. However, the court in *D.F. v. Leon County Sch.* Bd., 62 IDELR 167 (N.D. Fla. 2014), found that the parent who revoked her son's IDEA services because of a disagreement over the IEP did not prevent her from renewing her request for assisted technology (AT) for her hard-of-hearing son under the protections of 504 and the ADA.

Complaint Process/Enforcement

The IDEA is monitored by state boards of education through the due process hearing procedures and the Office of Special Education Programs (OSEP). Appeals are addressed in state or federal court.

Section 504 requires districts with 15 or more employees to designate a compliance officer and have a grievance procedure to investigate complaints. Parents can also file a complaint with the Office for Civil Rights. Noncompliance can result in a loss of federal funds.

Dual Eligibility

Generally, a student who is deemed eligible under the IDEA is also eligible under Section 504 [Section 706(8)(A)]. OCR has stated that it cannot "conceive of any situation in which [IDEA-eligible] children would not also be entitled to the protection extended by Section 504" [*Letter to Veir*, 20 IDELR 864 (OCR 1993)]. When students have a disability under IDEA, schools cannot opt to provide services in a Section 504 Plan [*Yankton Sch. Dist. v. Shramm*, 24 IDELR 704 (8th Cir. 1996)]. In one case, a school in Chicago was found to be in violation of providing a FAPE when they chose to implement a 504

Plan instead of an IEP. They supported their decision by stating that the 504 Plan was "sufficient" and the IEP would be "too intrusive" [*Chicago Sch. Dist. 299*, 54 IDELR 304 (SEA IL 2010)].

Students who are eligible under Section 504 are not always eligible under IDEA. It does not mean, however, that students should have both an IEP and a Section 504 Plan.

If the student has an IDEA disability as well as a non-IDEA disability, the development of the IEP should address both conditions. The non-IDEA disability services can be addressed as accommodations, modifications, educational, or related services in the IEP [*In re: Student with a Disability*, 114 LRP 39929 (SEA VA 2014)].

Discussion Questions

The following are hypothetical situations for you and your team to consider and discuss. Important points and answers to each situation are outlined in Chapter 6.

Mr & Mrs. Gripe

Mr. and Mrs. Gripe are not pleased with the accommodations and modifications put into their son's 504 Plan. They believe more extensive supports are warranted. As a result of the last meeting, they want to file a formal complaint.

What are their options?

What if their son had an IEP instead of a 504 Plan?

After further thinking about their son's situation, Mr. and Mrs. Gripe want to revoke consent for his 504 Plan and ask for the implementation of an IEP. They believe it will be a better document as he goes into college and will afford him the most interventions.

How should the school respond?

____

____

____

____

____

____

The new 504 Coordinator requires that team members bring students' report cards and progress monitoring data to the team meetings. He says this information is critical to eligibility.

Is his advice legally correct?

____

____

____

____

____

See Chapter 6 for a legal analysis of these situations.

CHAPTER 6

Issues & Answers

"Skill to do comes of doing."

Ralph Waldo Emerson

Section 504 is a civil rights law that seeks to "level the playing field" for individuals with disabilities. It protects against the differential treatment known as discrimination. It is enforced by the Office for Civil Rights, which has jurisdiction over schools and programs receiving federal financial assistance. All school staff should be aware of their obligation to afford an equal opportunity to disabled students according to this law.

Section 504 has a broad audience and encompasses those who may not be eligible under IDEA. Given the increasing number of students entering the school environment with mental health and medical issues, Section 504 is a law that offers them a chance to have the same opportunity to be successful as their nondisabled peers. It also is more flexible in terms of procedures and timelines, referring to IDEA compliance as one of the ways to comply with 504.

Section 504 is a useful tool for both school staff and those who are eligible under it. The regulatory language, quoted throughout these chapters, is straightforward. Further, OCR has provided plenty of guidance on how to interpret specific concepts and requirements. Implementing Section 504, with the help of this resource, should be seen as an opportunity to advance the rights of disabled students and ensure their equal protection under the law.

In earlier chapters, "situations" were presented as an opportunity to apply the legal concepts that were introduced and discussed. What follows is a breakdown of those situations with guidance on the considerations that would need to be taken, as well as the expected outcomes.

Chapter 1

Situation #1
Sexual Discrimination?

As you walk into the conference room, a sign directs you to sit in one of the front rows if you are male, because males usually have a tendency to leave early for both scheduled breaks and at the end of the day. Hopefully, sitting in the front row will decrease this temptation.

Is this discrimination?

Yes, it is discrimination because the differential treatment is solely due to the gender of the audience. Gender is a protected class.

Consider the classroom environment where a teacher may ask the special education students to sit in the front row, even though it is not a listed accommodation on their Section 504 Plan or IEP. If they only direct the special education students to the front row seats, this action would be discriminatory. If however, they also direct general education students to assigned seating, then no differential treatment of the disabled students has occurred and thus no discrimination.

Situation #2
Smoker Discrimination?

You are on a job interview and are asked if you are a smoker. When you answer "yes," you are told the interview is over because the company does not want to hire any smokers.

Is this discrimination?

No. Although treatment of interviewees is definitely different, it does not rise to the level of discrimination because it is not based on protected class status. Smokers are not a protected class under the law. Keep in mind that different treatment, in and of itself, is not discrimination. Different treatment based on someone's status as being in a protected class is discrimination.

Situation #3

Preferential Treatment?

Your school requires staff to be in their classrooms by 8:00 A.M. every morning. A teacher comes to you and shares that she has a daughter with a disability who takes medication. By the time the medication "kicks in," the bus has left and the daughter has to be taken to school by car. This results in your staff member coming to work at 8:20 A.M. Your staff requests this accommodation but you want to decline it.

Is this discrimination?

Maybe. Several factors need to be taken into account before a decision is made in this case. The applicable law for this scenario is the Americans with Disabilities Act. The first consideration is whether the parent is entitled to accommodations when it is her child who has the disability. The answer to that inquiry is a definite yes. The ADA covers not only individuals with disabilities but also those who are caring for a person with a disability. The parent of a child with a disability would therefore qualify for protections under the law. The second consideration is whether the accommodation that the parent is requesting is reasonable. The standard of what constitutes a reasonable accommodation under the ADA is made on a case-by-case basis. If this teacher has a full classroom and is expected to be actively teaching her class at 8:00 A.M., then a 20-minute delay every day may not be reasonable. It is unlikely that a substitute would be called in for the first 20 minutes of every day.

The question of whether an accommodation is reasonable is only applicable when addressing requests from adults. Simply put, you can deny accommodations to an adult. However, if the accommodation is necessary for a disabled student, there is no reasonableness inquiry; it must be done. The Office for Civil Rights has said:

> The responsibilities of school districts under Section 504, Part D (covering elementary and secondary education) are not limited to a reasonable accommodation standard. If substantial modifications are necessary to eliminate discrimination, then substantial modifications will be required. [OCR Response to Zirkel, 20 IDELR 134 (1993)]

Situation #4

Religious Discrimination?

You hire the best applicant for the job but later learn that she is Catholic and will be observing all of the religious holidays and holy days of obligation. You fear that this will interfere with her attendance and attention to her job responsibilities. You want to tell her that you have changed your mind regarding her employment and that another job applicant was more qualified for the job.

Is this discrimination?

Yes. This differential treatment is based on religion, which is a protected class.

Situation #5

Hair Color Discrimination?

Your advance placement physics teacher begins the school year by telling the students that the material in the class will be quite difficult to understand. He asks all blondes to come and sit in the front row. He promises to speak slowly to them and repeat directions frequently.

Is this discrimination?

No. Although this message may be considered both rude and offensive, it is not discrimination. Blondes are not a protected class. If he had asked all blonde girls to sit in the front row, gender-based discrimination could be claimed. However, as this scenario is outlined, no discrimination has occurred.

Situation #6
Disability Discrimination?

You are the building administrator for a special education program for students with behavioral challenges. The program has a physical restraint component. A required duty of all staff is to participate in physical restraint techniques. In the process of hiring a new teacher, it is shared with you that the applicant has a disability that precludes her from participating in any physical restraint procedure. You decide that you are not going to hire this particular applicant.

Is this discrimination?

No. The appropriate inquiry in this case is whether, under the ADA, the applicant is able to perform the essential functions of the job. If she cannot participate in the physical restraint procedures as required of all employees, then her exclusion would not be discrimination.

Chapter 2

Situation #1
Transfer Without Records

Jim transfers to your district without any school records. Jim's parents were silent as to his special education status. You later learn that Jim's IEP called for 40 minutes per week of speech services and 30 minutes per day in the Resource room. Jim's parents now demand that you make up the time, in spite of the fact that they never let you know of the IEP services.

Are you denying FAPE if you don't make up the time?

The initial reaction to this scenario is typically a sense of outrage that the parents were intentionally deceptive. In addition, staff often believe that such deception should not result in them having to work double time to make up for lost service. Unfortunately, it is not uncommon for some parents to use a change in location as a reason to temporarily stop services to see whether their child still needs them.

Although you may make the argument that this deception exempts staff from making up the time, consider the person who suffers as a result: the child. You may want to consider asking your team to put aside their issues of fairness and focus on the fact that the student is the one who will bear the consequences of poor decision making on the parents' part and a possible hard-line position by staff. A suggestion to compromise in order to meet the needs of the student will likely be seen in a favorable light if this case goes to hearing or court.

Situation #2
Forgotten Parent Invite

Your new case manager forgets to invite the parents to the IEP meeting. They attend anyway.

Is this a violation of FAPE?

No. Although it is a procedural error under IDEA, it did not equate to a denial of educational benefit to the student or an impediment to the right of the parent to participate in educational decisions regarding their child. A clerical error of this kind, with no harmful effect, will not be considered a FAPE violation.

Situation #3
Incomplete IEP

Your new case manager forgets to write down 30 minutes of social work on the IEP and as a result, the student does not receive it for the entire school year.

Is this a violation of FAPE?

Yes. Unlike the previous scenario, this situation has a consequence that affects the student's educational program and progress. Compensatory services to make up for the missed time are warranted.

Situation #4
Inconsistent Data Collection

Jill's parents complain that after three years of occupational therapy, their daughter's skills have not progressed. After you review the IEP, you find that the goals have remained consistent and the data collection has been inconsistent. She has had the same therapist for the last three years.

What are the chances of a successful FAPE claim?

What are the chances of a successful compensatory claim?

The chances of a successful FAPE claim are strong. The parents will rely on the lack of data and stagnant goals to support their case. Even though having a consistent therapist is not indicative of stagnation, it would be expected that someone who had a long-standing therapeutic relationship with the student would be able to make progress. It is also likely that the parents will be successful in their compensatory claim and be awarded occupational therapy services to make up for those that were not given appropriately.

Situation #5
Right To File A Complaint

Joe's parents request a Due Process Hearing based on the lack of "meaningful (academic) progress" that their son has made while receiving Resource room assistance. The district argues that the parents were always in agreement with the implementation and services in the previous IEPs and that they have therefore given up their right to file a complaint now.

Will the district's argument be successful at hearing?

Will this FAPE claim be successful?

The district staff may be surprised at the parent's recent change in position/ dissatisfaction with their services, but it is unlikely that their argument will be successful at hearing. After all, the party responsible for delivering a FAPE is the school, not the parent. The party responsible for ensuring compliance with the law and facilitating student growth under the IEP is the school, not the parent. Parents are not always aware of their rights or the type of progress, procedures, and so on that are to be afforded to them and their child. They do not give up their right to bring a complaint just because they did not bring it at the time of the occurrence.

Depending on the data that exist regarding student growth and progress under the IEP, they may or may not support a FAPE violation. This inquiry rests heavily on the data.

Situation #6
Mainstream Jane?

Jane's parents want her fully mainstreamed with her 5th grade classmates, despite the fact that she is functionally and cognitively at a prekindergarten level. The district believes that she is appropriately placed in the life skills class with peers who are at her ability level. This case will definitely go to due process if not resolved.

What is the LRE?

An important inquiry in the LRE determination, and one that is often overlooked, is whether the student is able to obtain educational benefit in the program or environment. The LRE needs to be a setting where FAPE can be delivered. After identifying the environments that might be appropriate, the team must look to those settings that offer the disabled student the maximum exposure to nondisabled peers.

In this case, a fully mainstreamed classroom is not capable of delivering FAPE. The needs of the student seem to be beyond the level of accommodations and curricular modifications. Mere inclusion with nondisabled peers is not enough to qualify as the LRE; the student must be afforded their right to a FAPE.

Situation #7
1:1 Aides

Your district is in a tough financial crisis. To cut down on the number of 1:1 aides that you employ, students who were previously given an aide for inclusion opportunities are now expected to either go alone or stay in the special education classroom. You have heard rumblings of a class action complaint by the parents.

Is this a violation of LRE?

Yes. Decreasing service due to financial issues violates both the IDEA as well as Section 504. The "F" in FAPE stands for free to the parents, not the school. Whatever supports are necessary to enable the student to receive their FAPE must be provided.

Situation #8
Home School Curriculum

According to his IEP, Todd needs a life skills curriculum and a variety of related services. However, the special education classroom that offers the curriculum and services is located in a different school within the district. Todd's parents request that the curriculum and services be replicated in his home school and argue that it is the least restrictive environment.

What is the LRE?

Do you have to replicate programs?

A factor in the LRE decision does include, especially when multiple locations are available, consideration of the distance from home school and community. The general idea is to keep the student with peers in the neighborhood or community when at all possible. It does not mean however, that schools need to replicate special education programs in each of their locations. An abundance of case law on the issue of program location is available, with the vast majority of them ruling that while the preference is for the home school, replication is not necessary.

Situation #9
Outside Placement

Mark is an emotionally disturbed student in your school. Staff members have exhausted their strategies and options for keeping him in the building and are now considering an outside placement. The parent agrees with this decision. You are confident that the cooperative program will meet Mark's needs but the parent wants a private therapeutic school. The parent's advocate has left a message for you to call her back.

What are your options?

What is the LRE?

The appropriate inquiry when looking at educational options should be focused on where the student can receive a FAPE. If the cooperative program and the private therapeutic school can both meet the student's needs, then the LRE factor regarding the site being the closest to home and community will prevail. In addition, it is more likely that the cooperative program will have other students who may also be from the student's community, which is another LRE factor. It is more likely that the cooperative program, if it can deliver a FAPE to this particular student, constitutes the LRE.

CHAPTER 3

Situation #1
Diabetes

Lisa is a student with diabetes. She was recently diagnosed, and her condition is unstable. She frequently misses class to eat her snack, check her blood sugar, and occasionally adjust her insulin dosage.

Is Lisa eligible under Section 504?

Yes. Lisa is eligible under Section 504. She should have a formal 504 Plan that outlines her needs and the supports that will be delivered to her.

Situation #2
ADHD

Tim is a student with ADHD. He takes a time-released medication at home and never requires medical supervision during the school day. Until recently, the school never knew of Tim's ADHD status. Tim's parents recently came to the school district and requested a Section 504 Plan. They said it will assist him in getting a better score on his upcoming ACT. As you review Tim's file, including his academic and disciplinary history, you see nothing remarkable. In fact, Tim is an exemplary student with average to above-average grades.

Is Tim eligible under Section 504?

Despite the parent's report of Tim's ADHD and even with supporting medical documentation that may identify him as having this condition, Tim does not exhibit any behavioral or performance issues that would indicate that he is substantially limited in a major life activity.

As a conservative approach, you may want to go through the evaluation process and gather information from a variety of sources. You could then sit down with the parent and show them the data that support that Tim does not qualify.

Another option would be to merely tell Tim's parents that the data do not support going forward with an evaluation. In either case, the parent should be given a copy of their procedural safeguards so that if they choose to pursue a grievance or complaint, they have the necessary information with which to do so.

Situation #3
Sexuality

Joseph has just "come out" with his sexuality. In sharing this information with his classmates, he is taunted mercilessly. His lawyer contacts the district and alleges a possible suit based on harassment and discrimination.

Is Joseph eligible under Section 504?

If not, what type of case is this and what is your plan of action?

No. Joseph is not disabled due to his sexual orientation. However, this situation needs to be addressed under your sexual harassment and bullying policies. When dealing with sexual harassment cases, the standard that the courts use is "deliberate indifference." This standard means different things to different judges and for this reason, you may want to err on the side of a consequence with a larger impact. Included in your actions should be professional development with staff on bullying and sexual harassment and school-wide efforts to address bullying.

Situation #4
Sports Injury

Rebecca has a cheerleading injury that requires her to have surgery and pins in her leg. She will be on crutches for at least 7 months. Teachers have been accommodating and have allowed Rebecca an alternate passing period, a locker "buddy," and an extra set of books for home. Rebecca's mother comes into the school and requests a Section 504 Plan.

What is your response?

Although this impairment is temporary, Rebecca meets the standard for a Section 504 Plan due to the extended nature of the impairment (over 6 months in duration) as well as the severity of the impairment. One might question why the parent is asking for a plan if the teachers are already doing so many accommodations. Many parents fear that if accommodations are not written down, they cannot rely on their continual implementation. Especially in situations of staff changes during the school year, a written 504 Plan reassures the parent that the accommodations will continue.

Situation #5
Peanut Allergy

Garrett is a recent transfer student in the first grade. As the district's 504 coordinator, you are contacted by Garrett's mother who insists on a meeting to set up a 504 Plan for her son. She brings in medical documentation of Garrett's fatal peanut allergy. She has a laundry list of classroom accommodations and environmental changes that will have to be made in order for Garrett to be safe in the school environment.

Is Garrett eligible under Section 504?

Yes. Garrett is eligible under Section 504. His allergy is an impairment that affects him in the major life activity of breathing. Plans addressing peanut allergies are often extremely critical, and procedures to ensure that all staff working with Garrett have the information is key.

Situation #6
AIDS

As the building administrator, you learn of a student's recent AIDS diagnosis. The student is not currently compromised by his condition. You meet with the parent to discuss a possible 504 Plan but the parent tells you that she does not want other staff to know of her son's condition for confidentiality reasons. She refuses to participate in the development of a 504 Plan and says she will take legal action if you intend on pursuing it.

Do you pursue it in the interest of school liability?

Procedurally, parental consent is needed before a 504 evaluation. It is also needed before a 504 Plan can be implemented. In this scenario, the school will not get parental consent because the parent is opposed to a 504 Plan. To pursue it in the interest of school liability is not recommended. The confidentiality of the student should be the primary concern of administration and steps should be taken to protect this right.

Situation #7
Accommodating A Parent With Disabilities

A parent with disabilities within the district calls and informs you that she plans on attending her son's holiday classroom performance this evening but will need preferential seating and a sign language interpreter. She wishes to be seated in one of the first two rows. The sign language interpreter charges a minimum of $500 due to the late notice, in addition to the hourly rate.

Do you have to make the requested accommodations?

The Americans with Disabilities Act is the applicable law in this case. The parent qualifies as an individual with a disability. Despite the late notice and financial hardship, it is likely that these accommodations would be considered by a court as being reasonable. You may want to be proactive about this issue by putting wording in your parent–student handbook about notification time for disability accommodations.

Chapter 4

Situation #1
Teacher Accommodations

After the 504 coordinator reminds the high school English teacher of her responsibilities under the terms of a 504 Plan written for one of her students, the teacher requests a meeting with the coordinator and the president of the union. The teacher claims that implementation of the plan constitutes a change in working conditions and, quite frankly, she does not have the time or resources to make all of the required accommodations.

Can the teacher successfully argue this claim?

No. Compliance with the terms of a Section 504 Plan is not optional. The teacher needs to be informed of her responsibilities under the plan and directed to implement them. Failure to follow the directive of a supervisor may constitute insubordination and be addressed in a disciplinary manner. In addition, the teacher's act of sharing student information with the union president may also constitute a violation of the student's right to privacy and confidentiality. The union president has no educational interest in the student so as to warrant knowing the terms of the Section 504 Plan.

Situation #2
Anxiety Disorder

Mr. and Mrs. Baker present a doctor's script identifying their daughter as having an anxiety disorder. They request the immediate development of a 504 Plan with the accommodations of extended time on homework, excusal for late arrival, and social work services.

What is your response?

The most appropriate response is to inform the parent that their request will be considered a request for a Section 504 evaluation. The evaluation process should be explained to them. Further, they should be told that the school would be happy to review any information that the parents would like to share, especially if the student is seeing a treating physician for her condition. Even if the student is found to have a mental impairment such as an anxiety disorder, a 504 Plan will only be appropriate if there is a substantial limitation on a major life activity. The label alone does not equate to services under Section 504. In effect, the parents' request for a 504 Plan is premature at this time.

Situation #3
Transition To High School

The elementary school district has a practice of developing a large number of 504 Plans for students during their 8th grade school year so they will be supported as they go on to high school. If students already have a 504 Plan, the minutes of service are increased to ensure success. The high school believes many of the plans are either excessive or unnecessary.

What action should the high school take?

This unfortunate situation plays out frequently between many elementary/junior high districts and high school districts. The intent of the junior high staff is not malicious; they want to ensure the success of their students in high school and believe this approach will give them the best chance to do so. Legally however, such categorical treatment is discrimination. The decision to develop the plans is not according to the need of the student(s) but is based on their special education status. The high school is left with the implementation and monitoring of multiple 504 Plans.

After the first semester, the high school district could gather the data on what services, accommodations, or modifications were used/ necessary and reconvene the team to discuss their continued appropriateness. It provides an excellent time for a reevaluation. After more data and input are received, the team will be in a better place to decide on continued eligibility and appropriate services.

Situation #4
Transfer Student

A student transfers to your school with records that include an individual health care plan. The parent is pleased with the plan and expects it to be followed as written.

What do you do?

This situation is contingent on the school's ability to effectively communicate with the parent and explain the benefits of developing a 504 Plan. Included in this discussion should be the fact that all of the components under the health care plan will be subsumed into the 504 Plan. The benefits of procedural safeguards, reevaluation, the role of the 504 coordinator, and the option of a grievance procedure in the event of parental dissatisfaction should be discussed. The fact that no disadvantage comes from developing a 504 Plan in this situation and communicating that to the parent is key.

Situation #5
More Than 100 Accommodations

Mr. Simpson has recently been told that his daughter, Lisa, has diabetes. He comes to the school with the doctor's script as well as a three-page document listing more than 100 accommodations and modifications that he says will need to be implemented. He shares with you that the accommodations document was obtained from the Internet as something that needs to be in every 504 Plan for a diabetic.

How do you respond?

A doctor's script alone is not enough data to develop a 504 Plan. Although Lisa undoubtedly has a physical impairment that substantially limits a major life activity, the discussion that is critical for the 504 team to have centers around the needed services, accommodations, or modifications. The Internet document produced by the parent is definitely not something that has been individualized to meet Lisa's needs. Parents do not always appreciate the individualized nature of the 504 Plan and believe that "more is better" in terms of the number of items. School staff should explain to the parent that categorically adopting all 100 items in the Internet document would not be responsive to Lisa's unique needs and could even be considered discriminatory.

CHAPTER 5

Mr & Mrs. Gripe

Mr. and Mrs. Gripe have several options for challenging the sufficiency of their child's 504 Plan. One option would be for the parents to file an internal complaint with the designated 504 Coordinator. This process should be outlined in the board policy/board procedures. Pursuing this option may result in a 504 Hearing with a hearing officer appointed by the school district or special education cooperative. As a result of a 504 hearing, a formal decision and order would be generated after a review of evidence and testimony.

Another alternative would be for a formal complaint to be filed by the parents with the Office for Civil Rights (OCR). For a successful claim, OCR would need to find that the school had exercised discrimination. The parents' claim would have to allege that more supports were necessary and were refused based on a discriminatory intent.

A more proactive approach for the parents would be for them to obtain additional information that supports their claim that their son needs more support. This could be in the form of an outside evaluation or report. Once obtained, the parents could ask that the 504 team reconvene to consider the information and make the appropriate adjustments to the 504 Plan.

If the student had an IEP instead of a 504 Plan, the alternatives would be different. The parents could ask to engage in mediation with the school in an attempt to resolve the issues. They could also file a formal request for a due process hearing. In that case, the state board of education would be involved in the process. The initiation of a due process hearing would include timelines for possible resolution efforts and closure to the case. In some states, a state complaint could be filed. In those cases, the state board of education would intervene to investigate the matter and bring it to closure.

What if their son had an IEP instead of a 504 plan?

Mr. and Mrs. Gripe certainly have the option of revoking consent for their son's 504 Plan. However, the case law supports the position that parents do not choose the Plan under which their child will receive services. Therefore, the school need not develop an IEP at the whim of the parents.

Unfortunately, Mr. and Mrs. Gripe are under the mistaken assumption of many parents regarding the most beneficial or powerful Plan to have as one goes forward into college or adulthood. Both an IEP and a 504 Plan are developed to meet the needs of individuals with disabilities. They both afford disabled individuals protections under their respective laws and are enforceable. One type of Plan does not "trump" the other. Assisting the parents in understanding both this concept and the protections afforded under the Americans with Disabilities Act may aid the parents in resolving this matter.

How should the school respond?

The school team is well advised to consider all outside reports and evaluations. This translates into reading the documents, comparing them to current information and even asking the experts who are present at the meeting some questions about their findings. Ultimately, the team needs to decide whether this information is relevant to making a decision about the supports that the student needs. While some experts may have more pertinent information than others, the team should allow the parents to present the information. If the case ultimately goes to a hearing level, it will be an important point that the school did not attempt to limit the parent's input into the process. Remember, considering information does not equate to accepting it.

Is his advice legally correct?

Report cards and other student performance information give limited information about the student and should not be used solely in determining eligibility. A perfect example of this would be a student with diabetes who is a straight A student. The student has a disability in a major life activity, although academic performance is not an area of deficit. The student may need a 504 Plan to allow for blood glucose monitoring, eating a snack, etc. The purpose of the Plan is to ensure that the student stays healthy enough to access their education and has the supports to do so. The student should not be penalized due to their high academic performance. Therefore, the position that academic information is critical is not accurate. Grades and report cards are but one piece of the student's overall performance.

Author

Christina Sepiol, J.D. Ed.D, is currently the Assistant Superintendent for Community Consolidated School District 181 in Hinsdale, Illinois. She has also served as an assistant director in a special education cooperative, and was legal counsel for numerous school districts throughout the State of Illinois, focusing her practice in matters related to special education, student discipline and disability rights.

Her educational experiences have included teaching in the field of special education at the elementary through high school levels and serving as a building principal in an alternative day school setting. Prior to representing school districts, Ms. Sepiol represented parents whose interests were adverse to school districts. She is a member of the Illinois Bar Association and has served on the Illinois Council of School Attorney's Committees on Special Education and the No Child Left Behind Act.

Sepiol graduated magna cum laude from Loyola University, where she received her Bachelor's Degree in education. She received her J.D. from Loyola, and her Master's degree in Educational Leadership from DePaul University.

For your convenience, we have established a dedicated website to download the discussion questions and answers. This gives you a choice to photocopy from the book or printing. The handouts will all be labeled with the corresponding titles and pages. **go.pesi.com/Section504**

References

Individuals With Disabilities Education Act, 20 U.S.C. § 1400 (2004).

Section 504 of the Rehabilitation Act of 1973, 29 U. S. C. § 794.

IDEA regulations, 34 C.F.R. §300 et. seq.

Section 504 regulations, 34 C.F.R. §104 et. seq.

Civil Rights Act of 1964, PL. 88–352, 78 Stat. 241

Age Discrimination Act of 1974, 29 U.S.C.A. Section 623 et. seq.

Title IX of the Education Amendments of 1972, 20 U.S.C. 1681 et seq., 34 CFR Part 106

Boy Scouts of America Equal Access Act, part of the No Child Left Behind Act, 20 U.S.C. 7905, 34 CFR Part 108

Table of Cases

Adam J. Keller Indep. Sch. Dist., 39 IDELR 1 (5th Cir. 2003)

Board of Education of the Hendrick Hudson Central School District Board of Education v. Rowley, 458 U.S. 176, 102 S. Ct. 3034, 103 LRP 31848 (06/28/82)

Brown v. Topeka Board of Education, 347 U.S. 483 (05/17/54)

Chicago Sch. Dist. 299, 54 IDELR 304 (SEA IL 2010)

Clyde K. v. Puyallup Sch. Dist., 21 IDELR 664 (9th Cir. 1994)

Doe v. Board of Education of Tullahoma City Schools, 20 IDELR 617 (6th Cir. 1993), cert denied, 511 U.S. 1108, 111 LRP 3215 (05/23/94)

D.F. v. Leon County Sch. Bd., 62 IDELR 167 (N.D. Fla. 2014)

In re: Student with a Disability, 114 LRP 39929 (SEA VA0 6/17/14)

Lamkin v. Lone Jack C-6 Sch. Dist., 58 IDELR 197 (W.D. Mo. 2012)

Pennsylvania Association for Retarded Children v. Commonwealth of Pennsylvania, 343 F. Supp. 279 (05/05/72)

Polk v. Central Susquehanna Intermediate Unit No. 16, 441 IDELR 130 (3rd Cir. 1988)

School Bd. of Indep Sch. Dist. No. 11 v. Renollett, 45 IDELR, 117 (8th Cir. 2006)

State ex rel. Beattie v. Board of Education of the City of Antigo, 172 N.W. 153 (Wisc. 1919)

Town of Burlington v. Dep't of Educ. for Mass., 555 IDELR 526 (1st Cir. 1984)

Yankton Sch.Dist. v. Shramm, 24 IDELR 704 (8th Cir. 1996)

OCR Guidance

Ansonia (CT) Public Schools, 56 IDELR (OCR 2010)

Broward County (FL) School District, 58 IDELR 292 (OCR 2012)

Community High Sch. Dist. 155 (IL), 51 IDELR 228(OCR 2008)

Dracut (MA) Public Schools, 110 LRP 48748 (OCR 05/27/2010)

Frequently Asked Questions About Section 504 and the Education of Children with Disabilities, 111 LRP 76408 (OCR 2011)

Garfield (NJ) School District, 18 IDELR 545 (OCR 1991)

Griffith (IN) Pub. Schs., 40 IDELR 105 (OCR 2003)

In re Report Cards and Transcripts for Students with Disabilities, 51 IDELR 50 (OCR 2008) *Isle of Wight County* (VA) *Public Schools,* 56 IDELR 111 (OCR 7/14/10)

James A. Garfield (OH) Local School District, 52 IDELR 142 (OCR 2009)

La Honda-Pescadero (Calif.) Unified Sch. Dist., 20 IDELR 833 (OCR 1993)

Leon County (FL) Sch. Dist., 50 IDELR 172 (OCR 2007)

Letter to Cohen, 25 IDELR 516 (OSEP 1996)

Letter to Durheim, 27 IDELR 380 (OCR 1997)

Letter to Ickes 305 IDELR 50 (OCR 1989)

Letter to McKethan, 23 IDELR 504 (OCR 1995)

Letter to Rahall, 21 IDELR 575 (OCR 1994)

Letter to Zirkel, 22 IDELR 667 (OCR 1995)

Maine (ME) School Administrative District #13, 55 IDELR 84 (OCR 2009)

Middleton-Cross Plains (WI) Area Sch. Dist. 16 IDELR 763 (OCR 1990)

OCR Response to Mentink, 19 IDELR 1127(1993)

OCR Response to Veir, 20 IDELR 864 (1993)

OCR Senior Staff Memorandum, 19 IDELR 859 (OCR 1992)

Pinellas County (FL) Sch. Dist., 20 IDELR 561 (OCR 1993)

Tyler (TX) Independent School District, 56 IDELR 24 (OCR 2010)